*W*hat Would *Nola* Do?

What My Mother Taught Me About Showing Up, Being
Present, and the Art of Caregiving

10th Anniversary Edition with Epilogue by the Author

Gerry Anderson Arango

First Edition 2014, SilverXord Publishing

Print Edition ISBN: 979-8-35098-242-8

Digital Edition ISBN: 979-8-35098-243-5

For Courtney Isabella and Nicolas

ACKNOWLEDGMENTS

This story is very dear to me, as are the people to whom I'd like to express my gratitude for all they did to bring my story to print. First of all, my undying love to my children Courtney and Nicolas, and to my husband Al who endured the gray glow of the computer monitor emanating from the guest room as I wrote and wrote into the night. Thanks also to those who said "Sure, I'll read it" when I sheepishly asked for their feedback, sometimes more than once: Claire Ann, Janice, Gaily, Renee, Rosa, Marybeth, Jenn and Ann, Betsy, and to my tech help, Mike, Sam and Dave. Thank you to Bill, my original editor. And special thanks to Helene and Joe, who are family to me now.

Additional thanks to Diane for her hard work and patience in bringing this 10th anniversary edition of "What Would Nola Do?" to fruition, and to the other geniuses at Networks for Training and Development for their support along the way.

Introduction

My House, 2011

Finally, a moment to talk to James. I'd looked forward to this all day. Curling up in my favorite old rust-colored wing chair, I reached to the left for a candle to light as soon as I'd turned off the lamp on the table beside me. The little green votive was stubborn tonight, almost burning my index finger as I inverted it so my lighter flame could reach up to the wick, now so deep down that I knew I wouldn't be able to light this candle too many more times. My eyes followed the dancing flame as I carefully turned the candle over and placed it on a plate next to the lamp.

I sighed so deeply that the flame reared back as if blown by a breeze from the window behind me. At the end of this day, I needed darkness to envelop me with just a flicker of light to discern the features of the face before me.

"You know, dear, sometimes when it gets to me, you're the only one I feel like talking to. I feel like I can cry in front of you, embarrassing as that is, and you won't judge me." I frowned as I heard my own words. "I feel like I can tell you things that sound ridiculous bouncing around inside my head, but I can make sense of them with you. Thanks for that. I can't always tell Al how overwhelmed I get with everything that's going on. I don't want to upset him, too – that's not going to help matters, and it would probably make him feel worse than me. This isn't the kind of stuff that is an easy fix, and I'm not sure I'm having much luck so far."

And James seemed to simply stare back, head tilted, eyes fixed on me.

"And I want everything to be all right, the kids, my mom and dad, everything. I feel like you're okay finally, but there's so much I still need to take care of."

James's gaze remained intense, as always, his expression serious. He always seemed to say more through the look in his eyes than the smile on his face anyway. Staring silently was not unusual for James. He had always been one to show his concern rather than talk about it, so I knew I didn't need looks or talk; I needed to feel like someone was listening.

I smiled, looking into his eyes. "Stick by me, okay?"

We had been friends for almost 20 years, James and I, but I don't think I'd ever felt closer to him than in the last year. He had shown me his support in what seemed to be a million little ways in the last 12 months, by what I can only describe as being there for me. Being there, remembering me at times he knew I was struggling, and sending a message of encouragement like dedicating a song whose words had meaning to me when he knew I'd be in the car listening to the radio. Being there. Little anonymous gifts that cheered me up when I least expected them, though I knew who they were from anyway. Always a surprise, always a comfort, James's many little gestures of friendship and support meant the world to me, and they made me smile like nothing else had this year.

I thought sadly about how the end of the week would mark that my dear James had been dead a whole year. I could never forget how he supported me in life, and I sometimes found myself still drawing on that care in a different way now, even in his passing.

My life, however, was going on.

I took one last look at the photo of James on the table beside me, blew out the candle, and stood up to answer the phone I could hear ringing in my bedroom. Someone picked up the downstairs line before I could make it to my room. My husband Al called up to me from the bottom of the stairs,

"Gerry! It's your mother!"

I raised my eyes to the ceiling as I walked out of the room. "Pray for me, James," I whispered. "I don't know what I'm going to say to her this time."

I ran my hand along the table at the bedroom door rather than turning on the light to find the phone. I stood in the dark, phone in hand, and squinted at the name on the caller ID before putting the phone to my ear. I leaned against the doorway, my head suddenly heavy on my neck.

"Hey, Mu," I said in a slightly louder, slower than usual voice. "Mu," as I call my mother Nola, often seemed unable to hear me at a normal volume these days, so I knew I had to snap out of my reflective state. "How are you doing?" Asking that question did not usually mark the beginning of a small talk kind of thing as it once did, so I instantly wished I had asked a different question.

"Oh, Gerry," she said sadly, "I don't know what's happening to me. I've been in bed all day." She paused. "My God, I just don't know what's going on with me."

And immediately, there we were in this place where word and thought would fail me yet again. Unable, as always, to turn the conversation or the situation around from this lament, I listened. I could hear pain in her voice and a picture of her materialized in my head, a frail little woman stretched out in her bed in the cotton floral pajamas she had not taken off all day. My mind raced for the right words, but finding none, I still had to respond with something. I leaned further into the door.

"Oh my," I sighed. "Have you eaten or anything?"

"I don't remember," she replied. "I think I had a cup of coffee, and your father made me toast or something."

"Well, that sounds like breakfast," I said. "That was a long time ago. Please, could you go eat something?" What could I tell her from thirty miles away that would actually help?

"Okay. I'll think about it." She paused again. "Can you come over?"

"It's ten o'clock at night, Mu. I can't come over now." This was the request I fought with. What good would driving to her house do to help the situation? Someone coming over cheered her up, certainly, and she would get out of bed if she had a visitor. Problem was, once the visitor left, back into bed she inevitably went.

"Well," I continued, realizing it might be better to give in this time, "maybe I can come tomorrow if Al can stay with the kids. Then we can talk a bit, okay?"

She brightened slightly. "That would be nice. So I'll see you tomorrow?"

"Sure," I answered. "I'll see you then."

I hung up the phone and raised my eyes to the ceiling once again. "This is what I'm talking about, James."

And what on earth was I doing telling my troubles to a photograph anyway? Was I that hard up for someone to listen? Actually, no. I was not. I had a small but dependable number of friends, good friends; friends who listened and cared. Some were even going through the elderly parent struggle themselves or had gone through it already and had wisdom to share. I was close to my sister and brother, and I had a husband who thought of my parents as his own. I was certainly not lacking support.

Maybe I just needed something more.

I continued into the dark room and flopped onto my bed, stretching myself out across the cool sheets, my arms and head dangling over the side. The blackness of the room gently softened into shades of gray as my eyes adjusted to streaks of white filtering in from the streetlights outside. In the distance, I could hear my son's voice coming from his bedroom. Oh, why wasn't he sleeping yet? And my daughter, the night owl – I needed to go tell her to shut off the TV and get some sleep. I pushed myself back up and went back out into the hallway.

Lights coming from both rooms at this hour. How did I let that happen?

"Okay, beautiful," I said to my daughter, Courtney, "Look at the time. You've got a 6:00 a.m. wake-up call tomorrow to make the bus. Okay, lights out, TV out." My eyes followed the white cord that ran along the floor to some other technology tucked under her blanket. "Uh, phone off," I added.

"Five minutes, Mom" she said softly. "I just want to see the end of this show."

I rolled my eyes and tried not to smile. I shut her door, knowing I'd be back to check in ten. I continued down the hall to Nic's room.

"What are you doing up, Nic?" I said, recognizing that I asked him that question twice already this night. "It's time for bed. Lights out."

"No!" he yelled.

I knew it was going to be one of those nights.

Part 1 – A Little "Who's Who"

Nicolas, 1998

The first thing, but not the most important thing, that I want to share with you about my son Nic is that he has Down syndrome. The second thing I want to share is a bit about the essay "Welcome to Holland" by Emily Perl Kingsley. It is pretty familiar to many parents of children with disabilities, especially those of us who have a child with Down syndrome. I think "Welcome to Holland" may qualify as required reading when the experience of a loved one's disability enters your life – inevitably, someone we meet along the way hands us a copy, sends us a link, whatever, and we then become part of the great chain whose job it is to circulate this essay for all eternity. I'm okay with being a link in that chain, I think.

"Welcome to Holland" relates the experience of raising a child with a disability to a dream-come-true trip you plan for Italy. In preparation for the journey, you make hotel reservations, buy all the tourist books on the shelf, devour the contents of every website on Italy, perhaps memorize a few Italian phrases from that traveler's dictionary you found, then purchase your plane ticket and off you go. But just before your plane lands, however, the flight attendant announces that your plane is circling the runway to Holland.

Holland?

"No, no," you say, "Italy. This plane is going to Italy. I am going to Italy."

Kingsley writes that the shock of this abrupt change in your plans is devastating, mind-boggling. You need to figure out very quickly what to do with this news. You know you're not going to get to see and do the things you dreamed of in Italy. You feel confused, heartbroken, maybe even angry. But in time, you begin to adjust to that which will not be. As you step out of the plane and you look around a bit though, you also begin to notice that though this place lacks the splendor of the Italy you dreamed of visiting, Holland may have its own beauty and its own magic. I guess that if I were to add a detail to both the Holland and the Italy of Kingsley's essay, it would be that though each place has its beauty, each place has its own rough terrain as well, expanses of territory for which no book, website, or advice column can prepare a traveler. Nicolas is both dream-come-true trip and rough terrain.

Nicolas, now 12, might best be defined by the word *survivor.*, true to the dictionary definition of somebody with great powers of endurance, somebody who makes it out the other side. I truly believe that had he been born even 10 years earlier, he would not have been born at all. Medical technology needed time to catch up to Nic. And people's expectations haven't always done so either.

My husband Al and I received the message early on that this child's life, if he lived, was going to be a detriment to our own, an inconvenience best addressed early.

. . .

October, 1997: I am sent for an ultrasound because my belly is larger than it should be at 18 weeks into my pregnancy. I notice my pants feeling, hmm, too tight too soon, remembering a smaller me at this point when pregnant with Courtney three years before.

I lay now in a darkened room, illuminated only by filtered light through the blinds, and the glow of a monitor, my Al sitting by my side. The technician, gazing at the screen as she moves her device around my belly, simply lays her equipment down and walks out of the room in the middle of the exam.

Al and I are left by ourselves in this darkened space to let our thoughts run wild. Why did she leave like that?

The attending physician replaces the technician now. He informs us what had shocked the technician away from her monitor is the sight of thickened flesh on the back of the baby's neck that suggested there might be "a problem."

"It could be Down syndrome," the doctor says flatly, resuming the ultrasound and gazing into the monitor, "or nothing at all." Furrowing his brow and turning to us, he added, "Or it could signal something not conducive to life. Would you like an amniocentesis to find out for sure?"

Well, Al and I know we want this baby, this who would be our second child. We had miscarried only months before.

Did it matter what this baby would have? No, but yes.

Did we want to know anyway?

We do now.

The doctor performs the amniocentesis, inserting the long needle into my belly and drawing out the necessary fluid for testing, then sends us home to begin the wait to find out what, if anything, is going on with our unborn child. I had been a special education teacher for several years, yet I wonder whether my teaching experience will prepare me for the possible lifetime commitment of parenting a child with a significant disability.

The other news, information not verifiable through an ultrasound back in the 1990s, is the baby's gender. We already have a daughter, and Al sometimes mused that it might be fun to have a son. You know, the banker's family, the matched set. Amniocentesis would reveal this information as well. And we could then look forward to some gender-specific shopping for what we hope will be a healthy baby. We also remember with guarded optimism that the doctor said the information on the ultrasound could mean nothing at all.

Still, there is the third possibility to anticipate, the possibility of a child who would not survive. I can feel this baby just starting to move in my womb, tiny flutters in my belly. How could this little one possibly die inside me?

The wait for a diagnosis for this baby is the longest 10 days of our life. Is it possible that each 24-hour day can last for 50 hours? Al and I can only hold on tightly to the bars on this roller coaster car, ascending the hill of anticipation as we wait for the results of the amniocentesis we consented to out of fear alone. There is nothing to do but wait and pray. But pray for what?

At the end of the 10 days, we receive the phone call we had waited for, for what felt like more than 10 days times 50.

"Mrs. Arango," says the nurse on the phone, "we got your test results this morning. The results indicate Trisomy 21, Down syndrome."

Wow.

The tests also indicate that the baby is a boy.

Wow!

Another voice comes onto the phone, now identifying itself as the genetic counselor. "Mrs. Arango," she says, "when would you like to schedule your abortion?"

Wow.

Well, our baby will live, and will have Down syndrome. So it's now time to get ready to learn what a college degree and a teaching job probably did not teach me about disability.

Our baby will be a boy, a little brother for his big sister. So now it's time to shop.

Labor begins two weeks early with a piercing pain in my back as my mother, Courtney, and I walk home from the playground. No time for an epidural at the hospital for this pregnancy. So nine pounds and seven ounces of baby enters the world in a hurry, with a full head of brown hair, and a pointy little chin jutting through the fullness of his face. He feels relaxed and peaceful compared to what I remember of my alert and screaming firstborn.

We quickly move into the rough terrain part of the dream-come-true trip. Nic is taken from the hospital hours after birth to the larger specialty children's hospital in Delaware. He's separated from me by 25 miles, because of perceived abnormalities beyond the Down syndrome. They tell us they do not think he can swallow. They tell us they do not think he can have a bowel movement. They tell us they cannot help him.

The hospital where he was born has panicked. It is as if they are saying, "We told you so."

James, 1992

I recently made a new friend who looks exactly like an old friend of mine from several years ago. This friend, James, and I had known each other for a total of 14 years, but we didn't speak much for the second seven. We met in the sacristy of the suburban Philadelphia church where he was stationed as an associate pastor. And for a short while, before starting a family, I made my small contribution to our parish as an alto in the choir and as a lector for Sunday Mass. I had lots more time back then.

James was hard to miss; six feet of blue-eyed prematurely gray Irishman with a husky build that seemed to challenge the seams of his graceful clerical vestments. I still clearly remember my reaction as Al and I laid eyes on him for the first time at the end of the procession of the altar server, lector, and celebrant at St. Theresa's, the parish we had only recently joined.

I leaned over to my husband that day, trying to not look as inattentive to ritual as I found myself at that moment, and I whispered, "Yikes, that's not a priest, that's a *Teamster.*"

James took his place on the altar as the Mass began, and his soft deep baritone greeted the congregation.

"The Lord be with..." brief pause... "*all* of you," he said. The *all* was not the usual script.

Al and I exchanged surprised looks – James exuded none of the roughness his burly appearance intimated. We would listen to him preach again and again in the gentlest and warmest of baritones, and with the most meaningful of words; heartfelt, insightful, and reflective of a deep understanding and devotion to the faith. And sometimes, for better or worse, those words could be directly reflective of his mood that day.

A good day" "The Mass has ended. Go in peace."

A bad day: "The Mass has ended."

What? No peace? Oh, fine. Be like that.

Still, the altar seemed to be James's canvas and his craft, the Mass, his preferred medium. His sermons seemed to speak to his congregation right where we were today, no vague or lofty references to put us ill at ease. Well-prepared, but not recited, often shared off the pulpit, as he stood right down among us on the church floor. There were occasional surprises like the envelope containing his monthly stipend handed off to someone in the congregation who volunteered to do some good with the money. And there was the sermon called "Don't Let Anybody *Should* on You." Clever and true, with an intimation of the vulgar, just for fun. I remember thinking, "Wait. What did he say?"

The stoles of James's vestments were often handmade – my favorite was the macramé – and each one had a story behind it. He delighted in the music that elevated each service, though he struggled to carry a High Mass or any other tune himself. James knew from the age of ten that he wanted to be a priest. Gosh, the only thing I knew at the age of 10 was that I was ten.

My early experiences of speaking with James one-on-one, however, often felt like being guest on a talk show. He was the host and I was this evening's special guest. I was peppered with questions wherever we met.

"So, you're not from around here?"

"What nationality *are* you?"

"Do you have brothers and sisters?"

"How long have you been working on your doctorate?"

"What's your real hair color?"

And of course, "How old are you?" —a question I was much more willing to answer back then.

Eventually, I became a bit sensitive to the one-sidedness of our conversations and my growing discomfort with the, uh, hot seat. So realizing I wasn't fascinating enough to dominate the conversation forever, I began asking questions back.

"So, you're from around here?"

"How many siblings do *you* have?"

"What do you guys do around here when you're not saying Mass?"

"What color was your hair before it turned gray?""

And eventually, "How old are *you*?"

James seemed hesitant to answer at first, taken aback by the sudden switch of the hot seat perhaps, but I persisted and he responded. It only took a few chats to learn about his sibling-filled Irish family and his position in it as the eldest of eight; the stint in the Navy where he refused to carry a gun and had to fake-shoot with a broom; his world travels, including the severe sunburning of that Celtic skin when he was in the Vatican at Saint Peter's Square; why he chose the priesthood (a question he said he didn't answer for just anyone); and about anything else I thought to ask. It seemed like he was surprised at being questioned about himself, like that wasn't the point of a conversation with a priest. I enjoyed listening to his stories, and especially the little parish gossip and cigarette smoke, as we chatted in the small yard between the church and the rectory. Eventually, the feeling of I'm being interviewed gave way to something more like a normal dialogue between two people, which worked for me. But sometimes normal dialogue could get a little misplaced, because like one Saturday I decided to have James hear my confession, but spent 45 minutes in the confessional having a chat instead. (I never did get absolved of my sins, and a very long line of sinners awaited him when I left the confessional. They must've thought I was in need of some major redemption. God certainly didn't find out that day. Plus, I emerged a little stiff from kneeling that long.)

Spending as much time as we did in service to the parish, James and I became more like friends than coworkers. We occasionally took our relationship out for a spin, passing time together out in the "real world," mostly in restaurants, as I think back. One afternoon, as he peppered me with questions over lunch yet again, I apparently impressed him with the fact that my sister, Gail, was the design director of a major music magazine. Just for fun, I began to slip him copies of the magazine she gave me, after I finished reading them. The first issue I gave him featured a topless Janet Jackson on the cover, with only her hands covering her breasts. And it was probably not the most appropriate magazine to slip a priest after Mass, but James liked keeping up with the music world, and perhaps his indirect connection to it as a friend of the sister of a very successful New York graphic designer. I smiled that day after church, slightly embarrassed for James as he stood in clerical garb, greeting parishioners after Mass with that racy magazine cover rolled up tightly in his non-handshaking hand.

This practice later evolved into the exchange of novels and music CDs. James loved music, bragging that he owned every Motown album ever made. He reminisced fondly about going with his friends down to broadcasts of the TV show, *American Bandstand*, at the studio not far from his high school, and escaping from Philadelphia to New York with his best friend to hear the popular music acts of the day. I envied his passion for music.

It was about a year later, after 6:30 AM Mass, as I prepared to leave for work, that I heard a flurry of surprised voices coming from the sacristy. Distracted from my own thoughts, I listened closer but could not clearly discern the words. Moments later, a woman came out and rushed over to me, the last person left in that corner of the church.

"Father is transferring," she exclaimed.

"Really." I said.

I thought back to a conversation that Al and I had with James one evening at dinner, where he casually asked me if I knew anything about Haitians, which I did not. He mentioned an interest in working with that community, but said no more that day. But now, there it was.

Curious, I stepped into the sacristy as he was leaving. Behind James were two of the women I came to think of as "the regulars," older ladies who always went to Mass, who set up the altar, who fussed over the priests like handmaids. From where I stood, they seemed a little flustered and weepy. I turned back from the sacristy to walk in James's direction.

"Ah, leaving us for Haitians?" I asked as we exited together. He confirmed that, yeah, this was to be his transfer, just like that.

"So aren't you gonna cry too?" He asked, as we slipped through the side door into the little yard of our many conversations. I wasn't sure if he was joking or not.

"Well, you're just being transferred," I said. "It's not like you're dying or something."

Which I don't suppose was the most sensitive way to say that.

James and I kept the chats going on even after he was transferred that summer, but I don't think he assumed such continuity would happen. Catholic priests who work for a diocese, as James did, seemed to me to be discouraged from getting too attached to people or places. Sounds like a safety measure, but feels like a sad one. Like it or not, you go where they tell you. Sitting in his living room one evening, James commented that he "didn't put nails in the walls," as Al and I admired some photographs hanging by the door. It's a transient lifestyle sometimes, I guess, the priesthood. In some ways, perhaps this detachment worked for such a life choice, leading men to focus inward, and to be able to give of themselves in personalized but emotionally removed ways.

But what does that detachment do for relationships? Does it keep you in the role of caregiver, always ministering and expecting nothing in return? Does it ask that you try not to get any more deeply involved?

Perhaps that leaves some men lonely.

James's new parish was as convenient to my work as a doctoral student at Temple University as his old parish was to my home just outside of Philadelphia. During those dissertation years, I often stopped by the decidedly more inner-city rectory where he was now stationed, St. Anselm's, before I went to the university to work on my research. On those Saturday mornings, he celebrated the Mass in the small front room to just a handful of locals and me. James and I would then adjourn to the kitchen of the large empty rectory for something to eat before I traveled downtown to lock myself in a room with my research.

One day, as we prepared to say goodbye after eating what became the customary breakfast of coffee and slightly burned Pop-Tarts slathered in butter, I asked him, "So what am I supposed to call you now that we don't work together anymore? *Just Jim? Father Jim*, like they do at the parish?"

He shrugged, "I don't care."

"Not even attached to your name then, huh?" I wondered, how can you not care what someone calls you?

Good little Catholic girl that I am inside, I decided not to call him anything until I could find a name I was comfortable saying. I never liked calling anyone *Jim*. I thought James was too nice of a name to shorten, so *Jim* got crossed off first, though that was how he was known to many. I thought about how when I spoke to James on the phone I would greet him by saying, "Hi, dear." And he often initiated calls to me in the same way. It wasn't too formal or too informal. It wasn't even a name. I nicknamed several friends and family members over the years, Nic, Nell, and Courtney included, just for fun. And now, another nickname joined the ranks. "Dear" worked for me.

Not So Dear, 1998

Over the next few years, James endeared himself to Al and me as the priest who blessed our first home, in the Catholic tradition. He was the minister who returned to our parish to baptize our two children, even though each time he had to travel back to our parish to do so. I came to know James as the preacher who made me think about my faith instead of daydreaming through sermons. He was the buddy who always treated me to lunch, and who Al and I, well, Al cooked dinner for, and the guest for whom we prepared the most decadent desserts. James and I enjoyed each other's company wherever the opportunity arose in the midst of busy lives and 20 more miles of physical distance than there had been before. But in the strange place between the church's expectation that priests remain detached in their relationships with the laity, and the personal relationships that can form despite this demand, James was also the guy who made a major mistake that almost cost us our friendship.

For Al and me, those first days in "Holland," adjusting to the news that our second child would have Down syndrome, felt like paddling a canoe into a dark tunnel. I could switch from expectant mommy to ball-of-tears on a moment's notice. We soon realized we needed to respond to the calls of family and friends to get together and talk, to plan, to worry, pray, whatever would help us move forward. As we made those phone calls, Al and I felt that our "family priest" needed to be there as friend and a spiritual presence as well. So I called James to join us. We didn't really expect him to do anything in particular, just to be there with us at the start of a tough time, and of course, to eat.

So Al and I cooked, well, Al cooked. We cleaned, we gathered my parents, my brother Mike and his family, my sister Gail, and a couple of close friends, but the family priest was a no show. No call, no nothing. In the midst of all the scared and sad already permeating our world, I felt hurt, confused, and just a bit embarrassed, too, sitting at the table with my family and that one particular empty seat at this one particular trying time.

"Who's that chair for?" my brother asked.

"Oh, uh, ju- just an extra," I lied.

Well, perhaps frustration, fear, or maybe the hormones of maternity fired me up that next Sunday, when I went up to James's new parish for mass with a few sentiments to share about that absence that evening, probably not in what we teachers would call an "inside voice."

I sat in the shadows in the back of the church, shooting little eye-daggers at James, creating descriptive new nicknames for who he was not so dear just now. This particular mass seemed to be taking forever. I didn't even take communion, choosing instead to sulk, all round and unseen in my seat. But when everyone else was gone, the very pregnant woman on the left was easy to spot.

James wandered back to where I sat after the service, plopping into the pew in front of me with a casual, "Hey, dear."

Well, heaven help him. Did he know he was about to be a deer in the crosshairs in this place where my fear, and my anger, and my sadness were about to take their aim at him?

"Mmm," I responded. "So what happened to you last weekend when we invited you over?" I asked in the most even tone I could muster.

"I didn't feel good." He shrugged.

Well, not a very satisfying response to the hormonally charged, so I leaned forward.

Eye-to-eye now, I left the fury fly in that empty church, thrashing him verbally in ways that only a stressed out, hormonally charged, somewhat irrational pregnant woman could. I think James recoiled physically like somebody hit him with a gust of wind, and I hope that gust was God smacking him on the forehead for being a jerk.

To my surprise, however, James was quite unaware of the importance of his absence that day. It seemed he didn't really understand the value of his presence to me and my family at such a difficult time, as minister and as friend. He expressed his profound sorrow at this misstep, interjecting, "I'm sorry, I'm so sorry," over and over again through my outburst. And though I told him he had done the unforgivable, that is anything that hurts my kids, even the unborn ones, and I may have slipped in a, "*What the Hell kind of piece of crap friend are you?*" He appeared at our house that evening. For some reason, he also offered me the futon that I once admired in his apartment.

I told him to drop it off on Tuesday.

James was by my side constantly after that episode in church, visiting with us, calling to check in, taking my two-year-old daughter, Courtney, and me out just to get an occasional break from my endless anticipation of the worst. There we were, passing time in restaurants once more, trying out decadent desserts, talking about Down syndrome, and about life as a parish priest. By the time my due date arrived, I think James would have delivered the baby if they'd let him.

And from birth through Nicolas's difficult first and worst year of illness, James was there for us. His presence meant the world to us. I recall with a smile the time he actually drove to Delaware to visit Nic in the hospital to be present with his very sick little friend during one of the many hospitalizations of Nic's first year.

"Well, I went to go see Nic, but I never found the hospital," James told us one night at dinner.

"You couldn't find *DuPont Children's Hospital?*" Al asked.

"DuPont? That's the name?" he said.

"Well, what were you looking for?"

"A children's hospital in Delaware."

"Well, well, talk about going on faith," Al answered.

It turned out James just drove and drove down I-95, stopping at gas stations to inquire about where the children's hospital was, though he had no name for it. He made the trip on faith alone. He hadn't failed. James never did find that hospital, badly marked as it was back then. He ended up fairly close to Maryland by the time he decided to turn back, but the effort meant as much to us as it would have if he'd found Nic in his little bed in DuPont. James and I shared the love of good food, popular music, family, God, and now his love for our very sick little Nic. A lot more time to talk, a chance to know each other in a difficult time. Friendship began to mean support, not just good times. It was no longer something *like* friendship, as I called it during the parish days, James was becoming family.

But Nic was barely over that worst first year when I noticed that I was hearing less and less from James, and being less and less able to call him, as well. I was busy with two young children now; Nic still not completely well, Courtney very busy with play dates and preschool. The medical dramas of Nic's first year had subsided a bit – for the moment. When I thought about James, I wondered about the purpose of detachment. I wondered about a phrase I'd once heard that people are in your life for "a reason, a season, or a lifetime." And I wondered for which reason James had been in ours.

Perhaps, there was a bit of method to what I thought was the madness of detachment. What do you do when your life's work discourages you from being more than you are to someone? I would only hear about the next few years from others. About where James was and what he was doing. The last thing I would hear of him would be from those same others, and it would be tragic. He would become a new friend, much the same, but different.

Nola

With all due respect to the acronym WWJD? or, "What would Jesus do?" I have an acronym for myself that reminds me of one of the things I admire about my mother: her effortless charm. "What would Nola do?" or, WWND? is what I whisper to myself at those times when my natural reserve and excessive self-consciousness needs to give way to a more welcoming, convivial, charming self; the kind of person my mother is and always has been. I use my little acronym when I survey a room full of strangers and it's time to join the crowd. I use it when I want to stop answering questions and start finding out about the person I'm talking to, because as much as I'm curious, I'm also anxious. Nola can talk to anyone. Nola can make anyone feel at home and always has a story or wants to hear yours. I'm not quite there, but when I try to think like Nola would, I get a little closer, one encounter at a time. She makes speaking to strangers look way too easy. I think that the trick is not taking yourself too seriously, and in taking more of an interest in someone else's story than in your own, if only for the duration of a chat at a party.

My mother has aged into disability, sort of an anxiety/depression/dementia trifecta that leaves her forgetful – sometime very forgetful – and always leaves her exceedingly frustrated and self-conscious about her real and perceived failings. Nola's ability to not take herself seriously has lately been compromised by her unreliable recall of little details and the big ones. And she knows it. Increasingly isolating herself from others now, it seems she also provides herself more time to ruminate in her perceived shortcomings and less opportunity to participate in the social interaction that makes her shine. Though always effortlessly slender, my mother chooses to pick at her meals or skip them altogether now, and of late has become small and frail looking, even in bulky winter clothing. The mention of a doctor's appointment sends her rushing to the counter to check and recheck the date, only to call my sister, my brother, or me to check on it a few times more. Nola is queen of the redial button. I don't think that going to the doctor is the actual problem as much as remembering the appointment dates and the times are – after all, to my mother, even talking to doctors is a social activity of sorts. At her best, Nola is still funny, sassy, and kind. At her worst, she is curled up in her bed, shades drawn way past waking time, silently staring at a TV, which always seems to be broadcasting something very Catholic.

My siblings and I decided that our mother's anxiety/depression/dementia trifecta began, or perhaps became unmistakable about three years ago, with the sudden death of her beloved older brother Alwyn, the last sibling left of her three older brothers. The changes in Nola were definitely worsened by the more expected passing of one of her lifelong best friends, my Aunt Ida, just a few months later. A shock yes, but not in the same way as Uncle Alwyn, for Aunt Ida had been ill for years. My aunt's cancer, perhaps, gave my mother a hint of what was to come, a bit of time to prepare for this eventual loss of a friend and sister of sorts., but Uncle Alwyn's death did not.

My aunt and my uncle were major players in my mother's young life, the people she was closest to, the family to whom she remained close emotionally, but distant from geographically as she left her native Jamaica for married life in New York City. Uncle Alwyn and Aunt Ida were the last surviving family members of her generation. This brother Alwyn, a Jesuit priest, witnessed my parents' wedding vowels, outlived all but Nola, his youngest sibling, and in later years resided quietly at Campion, the retirement community of fellow Jesuits just a few hours north of my parents, in Massachusetts. Brother and sister often talked on the phone, but Nola worried. Alwyn's health was deteriorating, his time growing shorter as he moved into his 90s. My mother and father were preparing to make the six-hour drive from New Jersey up to my uncle for a visit the day she received the phone call from Campion that her only surviving sibling had passed away in his sleep at the age of 92.

"Uncle Alwyn died," she told me on the phone that day with the same shock and horror one would reserve for someone who died young, suddenly, tragically. I guess we're never really prepared enough for death, even the death of a 92-year-old. My mother definitely was not prepared. "I am the last of my generation," she would sigh in this and many phone calls to come.

Nola lost her own mother, Lena, when she was just 18. My mother can still vividly describe the change in Lena's demeanor that seemed to appear out of nowhere, the change that began her mother's decline more than a half century before. Nola can recall her teenage embarrassment as her mother knelt as though paralyzed at the communion altar long after everyone else had gone back to their seats, the first hint of what was to come. Nola still mourns a woman once vibrant and in command, then suddenly silent. It was a change that lasted until the end of her mother's life.

"Mamma just went to bed one day and didn't get up," she told me as we sat on her bed one day. Stooped and speaking softly, she looked off somewhere I couldn't see, as though still puzzled by what she'd witnessed 60 some years ago,

"I was just a teenager. I didn't understand what was happening to her. Now it's happening to me."

Nola feels a great connection to the fate of her mother, though Lena was only in her late 50s when she died so many decades ago. My mother outlived two other brothers and a step-sister as well, plus many of her closest friends in both Jamaica and the US as she moved through her 80s. She now writes down the dates of the passing of family members and friends in the little red birthday book in which she once dutifully recorded their births and anniversaries.

It is a great gift to live the long life my mother has been given, but I only imagine that in some way the challenge is that it also leaves you more friends and family to mourn.

Part 2 – Nola, James, and Nic

Nola and Her "Nicky"

"When a child is born, so are
grandmothers."
— **Judith Levy**

Nicolas Anderson Arango came into the world with lots of drama and fanfare on the evening of March 3rd, 1998. Anticipating a rough childbirth because of the results of our amniocentesis, there were many extra checkpoints added to this journey into motherhood.

. . .

November 1997: *I am strapped down for targeted ultrasounds weekly in the months before Nic is born. Perhaps the medical team wants to know if he is still in there, and if so, what he's doing. I swallow disgustingly sugary liquids to test for gestational diabetes, though our midwife had correctly predicted that my largeness of belly was not diabetes, but rather "a big ol' fat baby." The doctors who insist on these tests seem compelled to prepare me, and perhaps themselves, for further unanticipated abnormalities and complications. In the end, I have neither diabetes nor a rough childbirth, but Nic's arrival into the world stirs up quite a bit of angst among many along the way besides Al and me. The genetic counselor at the hospital, who advised me when I got the results of the amnio that most people aborted a child with Down syndrome, is really just the leader of the band. A family member told me she prayed to God about the baby's Down syndrome, and that He told her the news was a big mistake. A woman in our church choir offers me her deepest sympathies at the news of Nic's birth. No maternity guidebooks prepare me for this pregnancy.*

The doctors tell us at Nic's birth that they're afraid that on top of the Down syndrome, our newborn cannot swallow and that he has something called Hirschsprung's disease, a blockage of the large intestine caused by improper muscle movement in the bowel, which is just as bad as it sounds. For these reasons, the doctors discharge Nic from the hospital where he entered the world and transport him 25 miles south to DuPont Hospital for Children in Wilmington the day after he's born. Nic lives in their neonatal intensive care unit while the doctors examine his little body from head to foot. I don't see my baby until I'm released from the hospital myself, two days later. Most of the babies in the NICU are premature. Nic weighs nine pounds, seven ounces. Positioned at the front of the unit, he is the first infant people see as they come into the neonatal intensive care unit. He looks like the bouncer in a biker bar.

Despite the dour prognostications of the medical establishment in two hospitals, Nic receives a clean bill of health 10 days later. Al and I are seriously wondering how we will ever be able to take care of such a complicated baby, this infant whose real and perceived issues caused two hospitals so much alarm. We drive from DuPont in complete terrified silence the night we bring Nic home. Sitting with him in my arms on our living room couch, however, he just looks like a really plump little brown-eyed baby boy with a sister overjoyed to see her much anticipated new brother. And that is kind of normal and nice.

The respiratory issues come first, and early, causing desperate late-night calls to the pediatrician and countless trips to the emergency room with a baby who cannot stop coughing in his own tiny effort to catch his breath. Eventually, to minimize trips to the ER, we are prescribed our own "durable medical equipment" for home use. A nebulizer to blow in steroid medications to relax Nic's constricted lungs; a deep suction machine to pull the thick mucus out of his throat that his low muscle tone cannot accomplish alone; and a CPAP nasal canula connected to an oxygen tank so he can get enough air as he sleeps – but no one sleeps because the tubes keep slipping out of Nic's tiny nostrils and tripping an alarm as his oxygen level drops. A hospital stay of a couple days here and there to get his breathing under control from this condition they call "stridor" becomes a common occurrence. Then at six months comes a strange tic that our pediatrician dismisses as, uh, a "leftover Moro reflex," and parents too trusting to question why a Moro reflex thrust backward, but this tic makes Nic flop forward. These increasingly dramatic tics are eventually diagnosed as infantile spasms, a.k.a. catastrophic childhood epilepsy, so named because of the difficulty in controlling these seizures and their association with intellectual disability "which Nic already has and which I still believe exacerbate his already compromised developmental issues." Admissions to the hospital again and again become a way of life, a ritual akin to grocery shopping – if you did it in an ambulance.

The endless string of admissions finally culminates in Nic being taken by ambulance to the local hospital one afternoon in October. Al and I are both at work and Nic is transported to a hospital where he has never been seen. Al's dear mother, who speaks little English, is not able to tell the EMTs enough information as they speed him into the ambulance after responding to her call as her grandson gasps uncontrollably while she's taking care of him. Nic is later airlifted from that local hospital to a renowned children's hospital – but it is not the renowned children's hospital that regularly admits Nic. When he arrives at the hospital, we learn that the staff back at the local hospital where the ambulance brought him initially assumed that Nic had been physically abused as he lay gasping for breath before them. Fortunately, our neighbor works in the kitchen and vouches for us in our absence. The local hospital had taken a chance and sent him to one of the two children's hospitals, but they picked the wrong one. As I said, Nic came into the world with lots of fanfare, lots of drama. Too much drama and the wrong kind of fanfare.

. . .

Nola took two ambulance rides with her "Nicky" during the early years when the hospital was our second home. They were on the first two occasions that she willingly volunteered to let her darling grandson and granddaughter visit for a sleepover weekend so their mom and dad could get a desperately needed break. By the end of the first night, however, Nic succumbed to the same respiratory distress on her watch that he had with us. The result was the same ride to the hospital, except that in the 55 and older community where my parents live, the hospital comes to you. My mother was the one who telephoned us from the hospital after their ambulance ride, apologetic for not being able to do better to help Nic herself.

It would frighten Nola as much as it would have frightened us to go through an ambulance ride – make that two ambulance rides – with an infant gasping for breath, Nic still got the occasional sleepover with his "Granola" (get it?). She also willingly did the reverse as well, sleeping over at our house and taking care of both her little grandchildren from time to time. It's what grandmas do, I guess, but this grandma has Nic's respiratory distress, seizures and medications to think about as well as another grandchild to take care of and a husband back in Jersey to check in on by phone. When for a short while the sleepovers needed to be more regular so that Al and I could go to work, my dad drove my mother to the bus station so that Nola could grab a newspaper and hop on a Greyhound bus to be there for us that evening. I have a lot to live up to if I ever get to be a grandma.

The surest sign that Nola is facing some new and unpleasant challenges as she ages was the initial regret, and then the outright refusal, to take care of Nic.

The surest sign that things were getting better was when she tried to give it a shot again. But it didn't last.

2007: The Unexpected Return of James

"Every parting is a form of death,
every reunion is a type of heaven."
— **Tryon Edwards**

"Intuition, the power or faculty of
gaining direct knowledge or cognition
without evident rational thought and
inference."
— **Merriam-Webster Dictionary**

The word friendship no longer seemed to describe my faded relationship with James. What little we saw of each other in the seven years after Nic's illness would be better described as a handful of brief, awkward encounters more typical of acquaintances than friends. By then, it was late 1999. I mused that James never made it out of the 20th century with us. I was not able to discern an answer to WWND? – What Would Nola Do? – for this one, so eventually, I stopped asking. I did not have enough of the charm or savvy I admired in my mother, it seemed, to communicate with James that in my mind, caregiving was just a part of friendship, not the reason for it. I so wished I had Nola's words here because James's steady presence during Nic's awful first years meant so much to Al and me, and now he was all but gone. I wondered sometimes if James felt he had completed his reason for being around us – and I so disagreed. Life went on without long, chatty lunches at Bennigan's, and home-cooked meals with my family, without phone calls to check in, or the emails that were the interesting new communication technology of the day. Life went on without this friend who attended to Nic in the hospital at 11:30 PM on New Year's Eve because I'd called to ask him to come bless my son when he got a chance, which James interpreted as, "Drop your champagne and come right now on New Year's Eve night. In hindsight, I was glad for that particular little misinterpretation, which more and more seemed to be both the challenge and the gift of knowing James, and I was deeply saddened that my friend was gone.

I nervously stopped at the rectory twice that first year, but the easy conversations of the past were now formal and stilted. I found myself feeling like a fool for taking that risk. I wondered if Nola would've understood what I was experiencing. I took a stab at attending mass at the church where James was stationed, but even that gesture felt forced and awkward. Greetings seemed to start and end with little more than "Hi," and a good bit of squirming, so eventually, I stashed my hopes away. It seemed that there was really nothing to say anymore. My children grew older and forgot "Father Jimmy," their friend they loved, that always brought a little gift from the trunk of his car, and who seemed to enjoy the company of the little folk as much as the company of their parents.

My second-to-last effort at a contact, a phone call around 2002, yielded a story from James that stopped me in my tracks. He said that he came back from celebrating mass one Saturday evening to the lights and commotion of fire engines in the rectory driveway. Firefighters were concentrating their attention, ladders, and hoses on one particular window on the third floor. James's bedroom had erupted in flames from what, to me, sounded like some kind of faulty wiring issue, the entire living area and most of the bedroom consumed by smoke and fire. There was suspicion after the incident that it had been caused by a cigarette left burning, but though he smoked heavily, I knew James was just not careless like that. He lost all of his books, a few of mine, all of his vestments for mass, and no doubt, lots of memories. What do you do with that kinda news?

Me, I hit the mall. I filled a wicker laundry basket with all kinds of "stuff," lots of little practical, personal necessities like toothbrushes, towels, books, soaps, plus silly non-necessities like candy bars – but no cigarettes – to hopefully soften the blow a bit for James. I left the parcel at his mother's doorstep with a note, then disappeared into the night feeling a little like the Tooth Fairy or the Easter Bunny or one of those other types that leaves little things for the good folk. I had a chance to offer a little care to James, and I was happy to do it.

A few days later, James called our house to tell me how much he appreciated my scavenger hunt of necessities jammed into a laundry basket. The only other gift he'd received after the fire was a Philadelphia Eagles jersey, probably the last thing one should give a Dallas Cowboys fan. We talked about getting together about where to eat and when, but neither of us followed through.

About a year later, I heard from a friend at our old parish that James had finally "made Pastor" of a church in one of the rougher sections of North Philadelphia, a parish with a lovely name, Our Lady of Peace. Pastor. I was so happy for him finally achieving what he long ago told me was his dream. I sent a congratulatory card signed from Al and the kids and me, but since past experiences reminded me that we didn't have much to say to each other any more, my effort at contact ended at that. I imagined, with a smile of reminiscence, my dear friend performing his liturgical magic in a parish of his own, though I would never get to see it.

. . .

Spring 2007: *Five more years passed, and memories of James finally fade in me, too. I'm back working full time now that Courtney and Nic are school age, teaching in the education department at a small Catholic university in Northeast Philadelphia. Our family moves from the house where James dined with us and played with our children, in the hopes of finding better schools for the kids. We find a modest home in an affluent town and life fills up with balancing the children's sports and school activities against the gentle pressures to advance my academic career after years of part-time work to keep extra money flowing. Though I occasionally think of James, with regret about the demise of our friendship, we're no longer part of each other's lives, and I'm used to it now.*

But, that spring, for reasons I cannot fathom, I begin to think about James again with a frequency that surprises and annoys me. It's been seven years. I begin to feel a persistent sense that I should find a way to reconnect with him, but I don't wanna feel like a fool for trying yet again – I don't need to endure the awkwardness. I have my pride, after all, and it has already taken a little beating. There seems to be no trigger for this reappearance of James in my mind, no nostalgic longing for better times. Life's different now. In the springtime of that year, James is a fleeting but frequent burst of memories in my mind, surprising and troubling to entertain after all this time, but by the end of June, as the easiness of summer begins and I turn back into full-time Mom, I'm harboring a constant, nagging feeling that I'm supposed to reconnect with him — and worse, I sense that there's a reason for the feeling. I flat out choose to ignore the sense, covering my ears to the incessant sounds of the inner voice whispering, "Go find James." Though dulled somewhat by the passage of time, I'm still smarting from my perception of why he and I parted in the first place, still bitter at the feeling that I had been deliberately and effortlessly ushered out of his life, plus, I figure I got about as much intuition as any inanimate object in the room, so the voice is really just me, talking to myself, nothing more, 'cause that kinda "woo-woo psychic intuition stuff" just doesn't happen in my world.

. . .

I mean, how on earth do you just start back up anyway? What do you say after "Hi," when the other person barely returns the greeting and his face turns crimson when you try?

The voice, still persistent, begins to emanate from new sources in the months that follow. I begin to hear James's name in unexpected places, from unexpected people. During the announcements at my church one Sunday, that same summer, the pastor announced to the congregation, "Our own Father Ishmael is going to be Pastor of Our Lady of Peace."

"Wait, that name sounds familiar," I think from my seat in the back. But, anyone who looks at the signs in the front of a Catholic church will see that there are lots of Our Lady of This', Our Lady of That's. And some of those "Our Lady of ___s are pretty common parish names. So, I dismiss my hunch.

The pastor pauses as his flock digests this news. "That's in North Philadelphia!" he adds, perhaps to jolt his affluent suburban parishioners by emphasizing that this guy was going into the "hood." Raising my eyebrows, I internalized that bit of clarification, and I wonder about not just what I'm hearing, but why.

So, after mass, I linger at the end of the greeting line to have a moment with my pastor.

"What happened to the current pastor up at Our Lady of Peace?" I ask.

"Health issues, I think," is the answer. "I believe he was too sick to stay in the job."

Sick? So, where was James now?

Well, *Ask and ye shall receive*, says the Good Book.

Several weeks later, as I sit working at my office computer, a coworker at the university pokes her head in and simply says, with her usual smile that James has returned to the parish where she'd worked with him years back – the parish I pass daily on my way to work – to "lend a hand." This said, she turns back in the direction of her office, and she's gone. Okay, another clarification I have not solicited. And once again, James is stationed just five miles from my job, two exits south on I-95.

Still, I wrestle against the urge to reconnect. I'm no longer "dear" to James after all, but it's as though the voice is louder and louder anyway.

"Go find James," it says. I cover my ears more tightly each time I hear the words.

Reluctantly, or because, perhaps, I just have to stop the noise in my head, I begin to soften and let myself reconsider. Is there something I can do without making a fool of myself? I mull over ways to silence the voice without further wounding my pride. James always loved my children – why not bring them for a visit? Nic and Courtney are traveling with me to work that summer to attend a reading clinic on campus. That would be harmless, just show up one day on the way home. But, I always find an excuse to put it off for another day, and when there isn't an easily available excuse, I just continue to cover my ears, shut my eyes tight and go, "La-la-la-la-la," loud enough to drown out the noise. I still can't muster Nola's charm to get me to the rectory door. June, July, and August roll into autumn, and I do not pull off I-95 to try to connect one more time, but the voice grows louder. *"Go find James. Go find James."* I can't stand it anymore. I can't "la la la" loud enough.

So, returning from work on a Tuesday afternoon in September with about a half hour to kill before meeting a friend for lunch, I find myself sliding into a parking space in front of the rectory to which James has supposedly returned. "It's on the way to my girlfriend's house," I remind myself, feeling a certain inevitability in my choice of taking a local street over the highway.

Seek and ye shall find.

I sit in the car and stare at the stone building, at once drawn to and repelled by the idea of walking to the door. "Go ahead, it's been calling you all summer," I taunt myself. "Go ahead. Walk toward another uncomfortable encounter, bursting with potential for more complete embarrassment and rejection, ya priest groupie." Who wouldn't look forward to that?

I open my car door and step out into the breezy autumn afternoon. I resist the immediate urge to fling myself back in the driver's seat, shut the door behind me and hit the gas. I take a step forward instead, click the lock with my key chain, and try my best not to look back.

As I walk along what feels like five uphill cobblestone miles to the rectory door, I pull out my cell phone and dial my very understanding friend Marybeth, asking her to just start talking to me so I don't think twice and turn back. She goes along with it, thankfully, distracting me with the usual, "How are you, doll" banter that starts a conversation, indulging me in this ridiculous request. It's awkward and embarrassing, and I haven't even gone into the rectory yet. I climb the steps and ring the bell.

Knock, and the door will be opened.

I greet the receptionist with a nervous smile, then inquire whether Father Jim is there. Her eyes widen, and she bites her lip. "Come in," she says, ushering me into the vestibule. She's familiar. In that moment, I flash back to coming through this rectory door a few years before when my car broke down about two blocks away. James was not in the building that day, but I remember this woman. I remember sensing that she was not convinced of my distress that day, eying me warily as she ushered me in so long ago to call their mechanic. The memory of that day makes me feel even more self-conscious, and just a bit ill-at-ease because of how quickly she is slipping me in now.

I hold my breath as I enter, nervous enough just from making it to the door at all. "Is Father Jim here?" It's a yes or no question, right? What could she have to say to me that I need to step inside for? The receptionist closes the door behind me, and I follow her to a small front office.

Turning back to me now, she shakes her head sadly. "Father Jim was in an accident back in the spring. It was horrible. He got sideswiped by a truck. His car was totaled."

"An accident? *What, is he dead?*" I think to ask this, but the woman continues.

"He was in the hospital for a month, in a coma." She closes her eyes and shakes her head again. "God, he was so *badly* injured." Accent on *badly*.

I had not listened to the persistent voice until that fall afternoon after work, and now my thoughts are full of it. Was that voice really a reason that I'm here now? It seems to me, in this moment, that the voice, that nagging feeling since the spring, whatever it was, had indeed persisted for some reason. It's still now, so I could listen to the rest of the story.

The receptionist describes the details she knows of the accident, explaining that James sustained a traumatic brain injury – a term I'd only encountered in textbooks – and a stroke at some point as well. No one knows which happened first. The accident happened back in May, just a day after my birthday, after which James lingered in a physician-induced coma for a month. His short-term memory has been short circuited by the brain injury and the stroke. The left side of his body is partially paralyzed. He probably won't remember me, she guesses, because she's been told that he can't remember much at all.

This news is so much to take in. I listen, incredulous. Words and unfathomable pictures of smashed cars and ambulances on I-95 flashing in my head like a bad dream last night. The receptionist tells me where James is living now, and jots down the name and phone number for me. I know the place, a nursing home only a few miles from my house.

A nursing home? What on earth… if that is so, *badly* injured does not seem to do his condition justice. If James sees me, will he remember me? Has he forgotten as much as she said? It's been some five years, seven if you're counting by quality. I have to find out, and I don't wanna wait long to do it.

On Friday of that same week, the day when I don't have classes scheduled, a day that's mine to do what I need to do, I take the short familiar ride to the nursing home. I pull into the front lot and park, once again stepping out into a warm fall afternoon, and once again wanting to jump back in the car and speed off from the dread I feel about what I might see.

I enter the nursing home lobby like a child lost on a scavenger hunt. I walk through a maze of men and women in wheelchairs, glancing from person to person in search of familiarity. I pass elderly folk gazing off into the fall day outside, some dozing off, perhaps in another place in their minds. Others offering a nod of greeting. I anchor my mind to my purpose again as I make my first stop, the sign in book at the front desk, and a receptionist who would know James's whereabout.

"Second floor," I'm told.

I turn to look for the elevator, and this first leg of the journey immediately becomes its last. Directly behind me is James in a wheelchair, flanked by his mother and his brother, Joe. I say, "Hello," stopping the trio in their tracks. In my mind, I also welcome his mother to Holland.

I'm taken aback by the sudden appearance of this man who has been out of our lives for seven years. He looks the same, but so different, thinner, paled by months of life now spent indoors, slightly hunched in his wheelchair. Trying not to convey the shock that's overcoming me, I slip past James, aware of his heavy gaze following me. I wonder if I'm anything to him but just another part of the background at that moment, a random passerby who happens to be staring at the relatively young man in the very old folks' home. I stop in front of his mother and reintroduce myself to this lady whom I'd met so long ago, placing myself into the context of James's past.

"I'm a friend from St. Theresa's parish. My name is Gerry." I'm a stranger to her now, but she takes my word for it. Turning me back toward James now, his mother bends down to him and whispers,

"Jimmy, do you know who this is?"

I stand waiting for a response now. Will the woman at the rectory be correct? She said he remembered almost nothing. She said he wouldn't know me. Why should he remember me after seven years, his terrible injuries and how we'd sort of faded out of each other's worlds?

I squat down by his side now, looking up at him as I try to keep my balance. Still stunned, I cannot muster a smile. "Hi, *dear*," I whisper.

His blue eyes look into mine for a moment, then up at his mother. "It's Gerry," he answers.

We move to a sitting area in the front of the nursing home, James, his mother, brother, and me. His mom tells me her version of the tragedy of James's accident, his coma, the months of rehab, the nursing home that is his home for now – this man, just 59 years old, his age doesn't sound so old to me, the closer I get to 50. And, looking around the room at his fellow residents, it feels even younger.

James's mother and brother slip away to speak to someone at the nurse's station. I'm left sitting with him, not knowing what to say.

"I missed you," says James.

And I return to my car that day knowing I will be back.

Survivor

"The race is not always to the swift
but to those who keep on running."
— Unknown

In his first years of life, Nic, this cherubic infant with the enormous brown eyes and the extra chromosome battled reflux, which caused him a discomfort that made him suck his fingers till they were pruney. He endured tonic-clonic seizures that medicine could not reliably control, and hearing loss in the left ear which resulted in at least three ear surgeries. His tiny lungs weathered reactive airway disorder which made Al and me experts at working a nebulizer. He suffered repeated bouts of pneumonia. Then there was the tonsillitis, the undescended testicles, and most alarmingly, the anomalid artery that was slowly closing off his airway. Removing this misplaced vessel would eventually require life-saving surgery, but it was put off again and again. Nic was rushed to the emergency room so regularly that Al and I each kept a full change of clothes in the trunk of our cars to be able to stay with our son when the doctors inevitably admitted him to the hospital. My husband and I spent our 10th wedding anniversary in the pizzeria across from the children's hospital instead of the upscale urban restaurant where we had made reservations because it's really hard to celebrate anything when your son is in an oxygen tent.

About a year ago, I came across a note I wrote at the beginning of our 10-day wait for the news of Nic's Down syndrome. Surprised to find this scrap of paper tucked into a book, I saw the date: November 7th of the previous year, and that opening of, "Dear God." I tried to recall what I could possibly have written as I began to read what I'd actually penned that day.

Dear God.

You know the anxiety that's in my heart right now. The news we got yesterday disturbed and frightened Al and me. Will our baby be "normal?" Will our child have Down syndrome? Will our child have some other chromosomal abnormality – one that would lessen the quality of his life or not give him a life at all? Did you hear what the doctors said?

Where is faith supposed to be at a time like this, Lord? Mine is failing me. Despite the odds, I choose to see the negatives and to feel betrayed by You as though somehow I'm "better" than all of this. I'm sorry, I wanna do better but this wart is beyond awful.

(So there's scribbling now, like my pen was skipping or maybe I'm taking a minute to collect my thoughts.)

Okay, Lord, take my fear, just take it. Please bring my family and me peace these next 10 days as we wait, and if it is Your will, give us a physically and mentally healthy new baby in March.

I'm gonna try to let go of what I can't control, Lord. Please bless us and let your will be known to us. And if it's all a big mistake, that would be really nice, too.

Cradle this child in Your arms. Heal any sickness that he may have. Stroke his hair, cuddle and caress him the way I hope to someday. Bless him abundantly and give him health.

Hold this baby's family close. Give us strength to understand and to follow, to trust and to keep believing. Help us to hear the positive voices that are You giving us peace.

I let go of my fears for this child, and I ask You to let Your will be done – for our acceptance of it.

Love,

Gerry

The first time I read this letter, its contents surprised me. I expected to read an impassioned plea for a "normal" baby and nothing more. I could still remember my rage when the genetic counselor took the phone from the nurse and advised me to terminate the pregnancy before I even had been able to share the news with Al. "Normal" seemed to be all that mattered.

What I read on that little sheet of notebook paper, however, had much more to do with fear and trust, faith, and just really wanting to have this baby. In the end, I believe I got what I prayed for. We did get to have the second child we wanted so much. Though the trip to Italy was indeed detoured to Holland, even as I read what I'd written, I could see myself asking God to walk with us on the rough terrain toward our dream-come-true destination. I cannot say, however, that I did a great job of "letting go."

In my opinion, anyone who could survive their first three years of life with as many ailments as Nic fought has already proven himself to be a very resilient individual. Our life with Nicolas continues to be a dream trip, peppered with rough spots, with friends we would never have met in Italy, with people who believe in our child, and people who do define him by his disability alone. Nicolas's life is a miracle of medical science, diligence, teamwork, and many, many prayers. I don't know if any ailment will ever do Nic in, but my husband Al and I, however, are a little spent.

Part 3 – Lessons About Life

"I am not afraid of storms, for I am
learning to sail my ship."
— Louisa May Alcott

Support Your Words with
Someone Else's

"To be occasionally quoted is the only
fame I care for."
— Alexander Smith

I earned a Doctorate in Education from Temple University in 1994, not as important an achievement to me as having children, and not nearly the work, the joy, the struggle, or the womb-to-tomb commitment, but certainly a life-changing event of sorts. My doctorate has led to a career in special education, six years on a government panel on education, some published articles, local and national presentations, a fairly impressive business card, and some really cool academic robes.

One of the strongest memories I have of the dissertation writing process, besides long days of typing in the computer lab or eating Pop-Tarts with James, is my advisor telling me that everything I wrote about needed to be substantiated by the authority of others. I had to have the goods, the evidence to support my hypotheses, and I had to be able to organize my research and the discussion that accompanied it into a coherent form. That discipline has followed me to almost everything I have written since. My first question after, *"Why?"* became, *"Says who?"* I also remember that the object of the whole process was to draw a conclusion and then generalize it back into the world. The final question became, *"Then what?"*

It all started when I came home from the nursing home one night with this déjà vu feeling. I was experiencing what I'd call "Nic moments" with James. Moments where what I learned as a mother was helping another mother's son. I also started experiencing "James moments" with Nola, moments where what I learned as James's friend was helping my mother. I started writing about my mother, my son, and my friend, in order to try to better understand what they were going through. I also wrote about what I'm going through in my attempts to be with them in our day-to-day lives. As I thought and wondered about the lessons I was learning along the way, dissertation logic began to take over. What did others say? What was my "hypothesis"?

Really, I just wanted to know more about Nola, James, Nic, and about me. I wanted to know about what we were experiencing together, and I wanted to know if anybody else had some wisdom about it to help me to be better at being there. I even wanted a better term for *being there*. I call it *compassionate presence* – *so* have some others – and to say that it really matters. I wanted to say that there is ability and disability. I wanted to say that a person can learn and grow while helping others do the same. And I wanted to ask God about a few things too.

So I'm grateful to Nic, Nola, and James for the opportunity I have to be with them in their life's challenges, as well as their everyday joys. There are no exotic locales in our story. We don't go more than 50 miles from my house at any given time. If this book were the subway, it would be the "local". Yet, what I'm learning has taken my life on a journey that's taking me far from where I started. I hope that my presence to Nic, Nola, and James is in even the smallest way the positive one I want it to be. No day is the same as the next. That's why I'm writing it down while I'm living it.

The Bathroom is an Important Place

"To decide, to be at the level of choice,
is to take responsibility for your life
and to be in control of your life."
— Abbie M. Dale

Nicolas took nine, count 'em, nine years, to toilet train. My husband and I read all the toileting books we could buy, borrow, photocopy. We dabbled in all of the tried and true methods, rewards, and plans, all promising a rapid, successful, and permanent farewell to incontinence. We spent entire weekends squeezing ourselves into our hall bathroom with Nic, plying him with diluted fruit juice to fill his bladder and rewarding him with crackers, M&Ms, and congratulatory toileting chants to the tune of various popular songs. Nic would make progress only to lose ground again in a few months and be back in disposable underwear. Al and I became toilet vigilantes, obsessively questioning Nic at appropriately spaced intervals as to whether he was "nice and dry," the language of the Foxx and Azrin toilet training program we'd memorized, and coaxing him to the bathroom at points in time that didn't necessarily mean as much to him as they did to the scheduled toilet trips we were making to plan for him. We watched and waited for bowel movements that came perhaps once a week after Nicolas held them inside for the entire preceding week. I don't know how he held it like that, and at times he still does this even now. In our frustration, Al and I would ask each other, "Why does he hold onto poop like it has cash value?" Toilet training has been much more of the parenting experience than it is supposed to be.

This witness of the betrayal of the body has become part of the new friend experience too. When I first visited James in the nursing home, it didn't take me long to see that he was in no condition to do much for himself, including using the bathroom independently. In those early months, communicating the need to use the restroom consisted of someone (never me) making a call to the nurse's station by pushing that little red button on the end of the long cord that was roped around James's bed rail. This call generally led to 20 minutes or so of sitting around waiting for a nursing assistant, who probably had seven or eight patients to take care of, and being a priest did not move him up on her waitlist. I imagined James's wait to be a much ramped-up version of that feeling I get driving on the highway after downing a large Diet Coke and I read the detour sign saying the next rest stop is 80 miles away.

In the months to follow, as James regained some strength and balance, he was able to use the bathroom with the physical support of his mother and brother, who visited him daily. I watched the two of them from my vantage point on the far side of the room, impressed by their patience and their agility with a man who easily had a hundred pounds on either of them. They were his family, I told my larger and probably physically-stronger-than-either-of-them self. Of course *they* could do it.

I spend a lot of time in the bathroom with males these days. Nic still needs some supervision to get through all of the steps in using the bathroom, but he's come a long way. In the meantime, Al and I continue to sing, read, and chat our way through many a week of constipation and encopresis, the almost French-sounding term I've learned for when a child holds his poop. Nic was so proud of a bowel movement a few months back that he asked his dad to take a picture of it to show me when I arrived home from work, and Al actually took it, another advantage of digital cameras and a bit of an embarrassing statement about what's exciting at our house.

Alone with James at the nursing home, however, I still cringed at the statement, "I have to go to the bathroom," for at this announcement, all other concerns became secondary. Conversation ground to a halt, and there were no family members I could hide behind. As always, the utterance of those eight deadly syllables meant ringing the call button for the nurse's aide, waiting for the aide to appear, and a certain amount of tension as the time passed with no response from the busy staff. It also meant sitting alone for 20 minutes when the nurse's aide finally arrived while she wheeled James out of the room to assist him in the bathroom; an endeavor so time-consuming that she would often leave him, tend to someone else, and then return to help him finish up. Minutes after exiting the bathroom, however, James would often look at me and once again utter the dreaded words, "I have to go to the bathroom," which often caused us to repeat the whole tedious ritual. Not being sure whether this second request was a real need or not, I judged not, choosing to err on the side of caution and cowardice. Someone else was going to have to take him to the bathroom anyway, not me. So I'd ring the bell again, wait for the aide again, wait around by myself again, then hope that he was done when he said he was so I could ring for the aide to come back and help him off the bowl. With only an hour or two to spend with James before leaving for home, this bathroom issue meant a lot of time sitting alone while he was in the bathroom, yet again, instead of visiting. But I just couldn't bring myself to handle the request any other way. And you're thinking "chicken," right?

It took me about four months to get over myself, get over my squeamishness, to make a somewhat selfish unselfish choice. It took feeling ridiculous and fussy and lazy watching everyone else help James but me as I sat there staring at the walls like they were interesting and trying not to get involved with this particular aspect of his need. Chicken.

In the end, it was mostly about James's mother. I realized the time had come to join the Take-a-Priest-to-the-Bathroom Club after observing her, a woman over 30 years my senior and a fraction of my weight, escort James to the bathroom by herself one too many times. Watching her wheel him in, supporting him as he stood, guiding him to sit, waiting, then so gently helping him back into the chair – she shamed me. Such love, such tenderness, such patience. What magic was this petite, 80-year-old working that I could not? Would I be embarrassed beyond speech at seeing a priest's man-parts? More important, would I perhaps lose my grip on him as he rose from the chair and cause a big scene and a lot of pain if he lost his balance and dropped to the floor in a big man-heap? What if he hit his head? But then again, how many more times could I answer, "No, I just can't," to the question, "Could you help me?"

Finally, after waiting for the aide just a bit too long one day, I gingerly rose from my chair and groaned, "Oh, all right," probably one of the most grudging and reluctant consents ever uttered to anyone. I think I even gilded the lily with, "But you damn well better not lose your balance!"

Sweet.

I can't say I remember how that first restroom rendezvous went, so it must have been pretty uneventful, and I've done it without a thought ever since. I'm guessing that I probably prayed that classic prayer, *"Oh-please-dear-God-don't-let him-fall-oh-please-oh-please-oh-please-oh-please."* I assume I held my breath the entire time. I probably got an unintentional peek at some man parts and didn't die of embarrassment, nd I'm guessing I spent a good bit of time staring at the bathroom walls like they, too, were interesting.

Over time, James and I have become comfortable enough, or perhaps too comfortable, to discuss various topics as we wait together in his rather large bathroom. It has become just another place for us to be, him perched on the throne, me perched on the sink. I'm happy that I don't have to sit around waiting for my friend, and I hope that a familiar face and a gentle touch makes his dependence on others a little more bearable. As we move through the rituals of the restroom, I often wonder what it must feel like to always need someone to assist you with this most basic of human functions, including, but not limited to, a woman you made friends with a few years ago at church.

I'm pondering the bathroom because beyond showing off my impressive restroom resumé, I think about how we all start out needing to learn how to do this very personal act with the guidance of someone who will eventually leave us to do it for ourselves. It is one of the first things we can control in our lives. Using the bathroom is a private time for most of us, and one made up of several very personal choices. What must it feel like to know you cannot do it alone, or cannot do it alone anymore? Did Nic or James always welcome the help or sometimes resent it? Is it an embarrassment or a relief? Is it weird to have to think about it so much?

I'm trying to remember not to assume anything when someone needs my help – I can't even assume that they need my help at all. When it comes to Nic and James, I at least try to step out of the bathroom as soon as possible so that they have privacy. Selfishly speaking, I still don't want to do this toileting thing with them. I will never embrace this task, but I have to be willing to assist if they need me, sometimes in ways that may be way outside of my gradually-expanding-despite-myself comfort zone. I have to ask, never assume, whether a person wants or needs my support. I need to let them do as much as they can for themselves. If, in this life, the only person you can really control is yourself, I cannot take away someone's control as I try to provide them help. If I don't keep this in my head somewhere, I'll only get better and better at toileting other people, the very thing I'm trying to get away from.

Disability Does Not Leave You When I Do

*"Do not try to fix me. I
am not broken."*
– Norman Kunc

I supervise at least five student teachers every semester as one quarter of my workload at the university. I observe all of these young women and men teach six lessons each per semester. 10 students per year times 6 visits each times 11 years is a lot of supervision (and mileage reimbursement). I take those experiences in elementary classrooms back with me to my sophomores, juniors, seniors and grads, hoping to help them understand their future students through my stories and what I continue to learn from observing on the front lines of education.

Somewhere during the fall semester at the university, I use my student teaching stories to remind my students in my classroom management courses – who are, themselves, getting ready to student teach – that just like a textbook says, children do not misbehave to ruin a perfect math or social studies lesson, even when you're convinced that they do. Children do not run out of the classroom to embarrass you in front of your supervisor. They do not throw their test papers on the ground because they are trying to show you who's really in charge. And when children are really struggling with work and refuse to do it, they do not necessarily need to be referred for special education services. As the students and I discuss this important concept, it leads us to the questions about why children misbehave, and eventually the conversation evolves into why children *need* to misbehave. I hope that the little addition of the word *need* begins to make my students think about the pervasiveness of disability in a person's life when it comes to how people behave, cope and respond.

Disability doesn't exist to ruin a math class or an art lesson, dear young future teacher; and disability stays with your student all day, long after you need to be aware of it.

This much I have learned as a teacher, especially in my first years, and as a parent pretty much on a daily basis. This much I share with my students twice a year when I run a video called *How Difficult Can This Be? The F.A.T City Workshop*. I'm showing a video, so I microwave some popcorn, I pass a bowl around along with a study guide. And the presenter, Dr. Richard Lavoie, leads a group of adults through an hour long simulation of what it might feel like to have a learning disability, and its impact on aspects of learning like processing, visual perception, behavior and motivation. F.A.T is an acronym for *frustration*, anxiety and *tension*. I think those initials about sum it up. I sometimes cannot believe I show a video that's over 25 years old, but PBS still sells it, so despite the massive shoulder pads and the moussed-up big hair on the women in the video, I know there's a great message here. Richard Lavoie and his room full of anxious participants never fail to make the same impression on the students that they do on me. Frustration, anxiety and tension; I take the message home, literally, in my son Nic and in myself.

When I send Nicolas off to school in the morning, he has a disability. Down syndrome is a disability that looks different on every child, although the physical appearance of a person with Down syndrome – the short stature, the almond eyes, the small facial features – is fairly easy to recognize. The cognitive element of the disability is more unique to each person, and on that spectrum, I think Nic's cognitive challenges are fairly significant. Nic has his disability at school, he has his disability on the bus back home, and he has his disability all night and all day long. I can see Nic's disability in his slow and deliberate movements, in the slightly drooping mouth and posture of someone whose muscle tone is low. Sometimes, I can see his disability in the way others look at him, in some children's curious eyes or in their subtle or sometimes not-so-subtle aversion to his friendly greeting, "Hi, I'm Nic." I can see that disability in the adult eyes of those who are sometimes a little more solicitous than they'd normally be to a 12-year-old. What? Because he's special? Because Down syndrome sometimes gives one an endearing child-like look, even as childhood passes? I can hear his disability in his speech, the difficult-to-discern phrases that those closest to him learned to understand through effort and with time. Sometimes I hear his disability in the tone of others, speaking in the slightly higher, slower pitch one reserves for a very young child, or in the voices of those who would ask me what he's thinking as though he is not there to tell them himself. I feel his disability when we are rushing somewhere and he lags behind or when I don't feel like subjecting myself to – or defending him – from the looks and the words that tell me that the whole world knows he has a disability and is not especially impressed. I see and feel his disability in myself when he screams and takes a swing at me instead of somehow telling me nonviolently that he wants out of his bedroom because the lightning is scaring him. I feel it when I know he's not getting any smaller and I'm not getting any younger. At that point, *I* feel frustration, anxiety and tension – that I am a card-carrying, mortgage-paying resident of F.A.T City. But Nicolas has a disability all day long, whether I'm feeling anything about it or not.

. . .

Taking my mother to her doctor's appointments at the gerontologist has become part of my shift in the siblings-take-mom-and-dad-to-the-doctor rotation of these past few years. I noticed something at my mother's last appointment with this doctor, a guy who made, heh, more eye contact with the computer screen than with Nola for the first two visits, but then suddenly became friendly and almost playful, which was something of a relief to me. I noticed that he also became more comfortable with using the dreaded word *dementia* when speaking to, not just about, Nola. The doctor doesn't say "becoming more forgetful," or speak of "a mild dementia," sparingly anymore. He uses the term *dementia* with no qualifiers, nothing to soften the blow, as though it is now appropriate and natural to use right in front of Nola, which I guess it is. If I find myself picking up on this new specificity, I wonder if my mother does, and how the word dementia sounds to her as a new point of reference about her condition. It's not going away, is it?

. . .

I sometimes wonder what goes through James's mind as he thinks back to a time when he did not have a traumatic brain injury and all those strokes impacting every movement he makes, every minute of his day. I wonder if he looks around him at the pastel walls and the pastel uniforms and the beige food and wonders how the hell he ended up in a nursing home at 59. Does James think back often to the pre-disability days, the days of sermons and beautiful vestments, of meaningful work, of driving a car, of sitting on real sofas and smoking lots of cigarettes, or is life a moment-by-moment struggle to overcome the fear of what's happening to him right this minute? Is it too difficult to think about? Will James ever get to go home, or is the nursing home the last place he'll ever live? What's it like when your memory is no longer a friend you can depend on, or when you have no choice but to rely on three different shift workers a day to feed, clothe, toilet and medicate you? When James's family or I leave for the day, is it terrifying to be in the hands of people who exist day-to-day in your compromised short-term memory, but may be strangers to you when they return tomorrow? What will life look like five years from now if nothing changes for James? After all, his disability doesn't go away when we do. I know that scares his mother to death. And to use a phrase that says it all for me, "it makes my head explode." But fortunately for me, that's just a phrase.

. . .

Other people's disabilities force me to slow down. This is not always a bad thing. Other people's disabilities make me think more about how what is pretty easy for me is often difficult for another, and whether there is something I can do to take the edge off of someone else's challenges if they need me. Other people's disabilities make me appreciate the fragility of life, of the body, of the ego. Other people's disabilities challenge me to try to be less selfish, and to be careful of being too selfless.

As I spend time with Nic, Nola and James, I want to remember that despite what goes on between us – in the conversations, struggles, arguments, whatever – I need to have the humility to realize that disability is not there to scramble a good conversation, nor to annoy, scare or sadden me, even when it sometimes does. Disability – Down syndrome, dementia, traumatic brain injury – it's all day long for Nic, Nola and James. What is said, or what happens because of the challenges of disability is nothing personal, even when it feels as if they are, and I am very familiar with that feeling. I generally think that the hurtful things we all do when we're struggling are not meant to be taken personally, though in the moment it is not always apparent to me as the person on the receiving end. In that moment, I'm just not that insightful.

The struggles that Nic, Nola and James own also make them who they are right now. They make Nic funny, warm and affectionate. They make him uninhibited and impossible to ignore. Nic's challenges make his every little milestone a celebration for us; our family takes nothing for granted. James's challenges make him brutally honest, sometimes in ways that can be upsetting to hear as they emanate from that pain within. But so many times that same honesty is a bit bittersweet, revealing feelings he may never have expressed so plainly before his accident. Sometimes these same challenges cause me to sit there in a little bit of awe of a man who has never given up his faith in God, despite the terrible turn his life has taken.

Nola, well, I'm not so sure. Obviously, I've known my mother the longest of the three, and her role has evolved all my life. Sometimes I just miss the mom I used to have, the one who ran the show, who made everyone feel at home, the one with the good sense of humor and the rather bad temper. She took care of me, now I help to take care of her. I look into her eyes too, sometimes, and I stare into the fear and the anger and her sadness. Perhaps they'd been there all along. That trifecta and all though, she's still Nola. Do the dementia, depression and anxiety merely intensify the elements of her personality that were always there, underneath it all? Maybe, maybe not.

Disability is all day long, not just when I'm in the room. I am reminded in Nic, Nola and James, that people are so much more complex than their physical or mental challenges. Disability is only part of what I experience about them, though it is always a part of the way they experience the world. Does that mean I have a firm grasp of the obvious? Eh, perhaps. But it's that part about disability being something of a way of life and not just what someone has that I continue to ponder.

Purpose! Purpose! Purpose!

"The joy in life is to be used for
a purpose. I want to be used up
when I die."
– George Bernard Shaw

Since I teach at a university, it seems I educated my way into having the entire summer – actually May through August – off. I feel very fortunate as a mother to be able to stay home with little to no childcare issues (but also, alas, with little to no income). I do find, though, that after a few weeks without the routines of school and work, I start to have a hard time remembering what day of the week it is. What my children do in the summer, they do on specific days and times like Courtney working part-time or volunteering, or Nic going to camp (I know because, guess who drives them) but what I do in the summer can be pretty much done any day of the week. I clean the house sometimes, I put tomato plants into the ground and hope for the best, I prep a syllabus or two or three for the fall semester to come. Once September rolls around, I will know Tuesday from Thursday again, but by late July, life is all one big Friday to me. There isn't much reason to care about such free-form weeks in the summer, but for me it is a temporary state. Soon enough it's back to classes, student teachers, the children's sports and clubs, and trying to squeeze in time for making beds and paying bills – in other words, back to a schedule that makes each day a good bit different from the next.

I wonder, sometimes, what it would be like not to have any particular work to do on any particular day as an ongoing way of life. What if I didn't have to be in Room 227, Education Building with projects graded on Monday mornings at 9:35 AM? What if no one in particular needed anything in particular from me at any particular time? How would one day be different from the next? Would it confuse me eventually? Frustrate me? Sadden me? What if, as my long-retired father says, every day felt like "Sunday"? From where I sit right now, it sounds like a little piece of heaven, but I don't know that it really is.

Nola has a gigantic, three-month calendar hanging on her kitchen wall that Gail got from a friend at *The New York Times*. James has a calendar hanging on his wall, too. His friend Bob brought it from the Philadelphia Mummers, an organization he belongs to, and it's got lucky numbers to play on it for each day of the week. Both calendars are fairly bereft of fun event entries for either Nola or James though, and I don't know if anyone ever plays the calendar's numbers on that Mummers calendar. At this point in their lives, I'm not sure if my mother or James use calendars to mark the days that one stands out from the next. From my fly-on-the-wall view, their calendars seem mostly to be a place for notation of doctor's appointments. I can't imagine that doctor's appointments alone can give one much of a purpose for getting out of bed, certainly not the larger than life meaningful purposes that they both once knew. And in my experience, doctor's appointments are rarely occasions to look forward to, much as I like my doctor.

My mother once marked her days by a full-time job, by children busy-ness, husband busy-ness, and later by the clubs she joined, visiting friends and family, the maintenance of her home, membership in the local historical society, and her weekly walk to deliver her retirement community newsletter. That level of activity has evaporated over the last few years. It seems sometimes that my mother's last real purpose for getting out of bed was after my father's first heart attack. During that alarming episode, Nola became once again focused, full of her ever-available charm, and intent on whatever she needed to do to help her husband recover. It was a great, classic *Nola* response to an awful situation. WWND, what would Nola do? Ask doctors lots of questions, dote on my dad, show up at his bedside every day, scold him for eating so badly that he gave himself a cardiac. By this definition, Nola's next purpose for getting out of bed will be six days from today when Nic sleeps over at her house, so that I can go to work while Al is away on business. She's up for it, and I'm taking advantage. My mother will be focused, will make sure Nic gets his meds, all the cheese and crackers he can eat, and she will enjoy having him visit with her and any friends who stop by. Nola will also remind him at strategic intervals to go use the bathroom, she knows the drill. My mother will be a woman with a purpose and I know Nic will so enjoy spending time being indulged – and probably overfed – by his "Granola".

My mother is the same age as James's mother and my husband Al's mother. James's mother spends hours with him at the nursing home, five days a week. She brings him baggies of little ham sandwiches on white bread, those salty little six-packs of square cheese crackers, and all the caffeine-free diet cola he can drink. She and one of his brothers or sisters transport him home on Sundays. James's mom is stunning, even at 83, and her close-cropped auburn hair is perfect (I add this in homage to the hair obsession of my mother's side of the family. I can't help it). Al's mother takes care of two toddler great-grandchildren eight hours a day while their parents work; I got to meet one of the great-grand kiddies because Al's mom traveled with the little guy on the plane from Florida to visit us in Pennsylvania, car seat, stroller, baby luggage and all. Al's mother doesn't seem to think twice about doing things like that. Plus when she comes over she straightens up my entire house and I never see her do it. She cooks at least two meals for us every day of her visit, and I do not resent any of this help in the least.

Unfortunately, my mother is aware of what these two women (who are her age) are able to do and she frequently compares herself to them.

"Oh, I wish I was like Al's mother," she says as she lies in her bed. "She can do anything. What happened to me? I just want to get back to being my old self." I then mentally strike "Al's mother" off my "topics of conversation" list.

Nola shouldn't "should" on herself, you know? I feel like I can't even compare to Al and James's mothers myself! Lamenting her inability to measure up to their energy level makes my mother feel old, too old, and more incapable than she really is. I heard the Jesuit priest and author James Martin refer to this as "compare and despair" at a conference I went to last year, and I immediately thought, "Mu! That's about the size of it for my mother."

. . .

I think that having a purpose, even an unfortunate purpose like caring for your husband after his heart attack or spending most of your time at the bedside of your eldest child when you are both members of the 55-and-over club, is still a reason to *be*, to get up in the morning, a purpose that marks your days and gives them meaning. Done right, it is the essence of compassionate presence, of being there. There are other types of purpose, of course; the cause, the art, the career to which people devote themselves. Some devote themselves to other people, or to the quest for knowledge and understanding of that which they cannot explain. I think having a purpose puts your brain and your body in problem-solving mode, makes you think less about the obstacles you might face and more about the goal you're shooting for, like a healthy husband or happy great-grandchildren.

The kind of being useful that involves others with challenges though, also goes by the name *caregiving*. Now it starts to feel a little loaded to me. I never really thought of myself as a caregiver when it came to Nic. In that way, caregiver and mother are synonymous, the word for what all mothers do to a great or lesser extent. Does being the parent of a child with physical or physiological or intellectual issues add additional levels of caregiving? Yes, but most of us will engage in the role of caregiver at some point in life as we try to support our elderly parents, our friends, our siblings, or other people with acquired disabilities — I just started my role sooner than some. I once read a quote from the Family Caregiver Alliance which said, "You either are a caregiver, will be a caregiver, or someone will be caring for you between now and whenever you die" and it really stuck with me. In other words, we're all either going to experience caregiver stress, cause it — or both. Caregiving is inescapable, then? I either get it, give it, or both? Well, I think I'll take that as a rallying cry and realize that I'm on the varsity team, on the giving side — for now. And as a "giver," I need to remember that flip side of caregiving — taking care of self — needs some attention, too. Getting all whipped up about problems at my mother's house, then eating four bowls of Lucky Charms probably isn't the best way to take care of myself. I still need to figure out what needs food versus what needs a lot of prayer, a few deep breaths, a *Zumba* class, or maybe a little Chardonnay.

Caregiving has a positive side — every day isn't Sunday when someone needs you, for sure. Having purpose doesn't have to look any particular way, but I think it gives life its meaning. My mother probably has no idea how much purpose she's served in my life. I won't forget to thank her for Nic's sleepover.

Social Skills Matter

*"Charm is the quality in others that
makes us more satisfied with
ourselves."*
– Henri-Frédéric Amiel

Outliers by Malcolm Gladwell is one of the best books I think I've ever read. I liked it so much that I also bought the audiobook for my car, loaded it on my MP3 player, and then I read it two more times and will probably pick it up again soon. Malcolm Gladwell, besides being high octane brilliant, also has a nice speaking voice to drive along to in my car. It's a book that gave me very powerful information to walk away with after I finished it. And every time I read or listen to it, I feel like I learn something new.

To me, one of the premises of *Outliers* is that there is no such thing as the "self-made man." Success in life does not just happen by someone's sheer force of will, and it isn't based on any one unique trait in a person. Success, according to Gladwell, has five contributing factors in all. Put this book on your reading list so you can learn for yourself what they are, but I can tell you that the one that jumps out at me as I write about James, Nola, and Nic, is that a successful person needs the social savvy to know how to work with situations and people. If this is a factor of success, then my mother Nola has always been a very successful woman. She has oodles of social savvy (from which I borrow in those What Would Nola Do moments). Nola is able to step away from herself and give you the spotlight, and people love her for it. Nola sent little "thinking of you" notes to friends back when doing so required postage and stationery instead of an email account. Nola's not the world's greatest cook, but she makes sure everyone has eaten well at her house, even if she never touched the stove. Nola makes conversation with ease and loves to spin a ripping yarn from days gone by.

These days my mom and dad spend a lot of time with doctors. Sometimes when I accompany them on an appointment, I witness the doctor-patient exchange with less of the tension that accompanies it when it involves my own health and my own doctor. Some physicians are warm fuzzies and some physicians are standoffish and appear to me to lack basic social skills despite their professional success, perhaps, in some cases, because of it. But Nola treats them all the same. She makes the same small talk, enjoys telling them what she wants to do to her children for bugging her about her health, and does not forget the fact that she is much older and therefore wiser than even the most learned but aloof physician.

My mother returned to the office of the practice where my father received his bladder cancer treatments with a box of cookies, as a token of her gratitude for their treatment of my dad during his illness. Nola didn't have an appointment, she just had cookies. No-nonsense nurses defrost and tell Nola their life stories while she's waiting for her doctor. I've watched the thaw. She flirts with the handsome docs. I wouldn't have the nerve. What would all this be like if she didn't have that social savvy? I think sometimes that continuing to cast her wide net of charm is a way to keep the shifts in her cognitive world a bit more normal for her. All those trips to the doctor – not normal. All this illness – not normal. Normal is healthy. Normal is friendly. Normal is charming. Normal feels like *Nola*. Dementia does not. Act as normally as possible, and life in a sickness-and-dementia world seems less abnormal.

Before James's accident, as we got to know each other and I watched him deal with certain situations, I sometimes felt a bit of concern about his social savvy. James was a creative, sincere, spiritual, generous man; it was obvious on the altar and sometimes fun after hours at the restaurant of our choice – but he seemed to misunderstand others and to be misunderstood by them just a bit more often than the average guy. There were two or three occasions where James told me about conflicts he was experiencing with people he knew. I found that I needed to explain to him as best I could the other person's seemingly obvious point of view. When James called one evening to tell me that he would not celebrate a friend's funeral service because her daughter was giving him a hard time, I reminded him over and over, and louder and louder, through his protests, that his only concern needed to be paying tribute to his departed friend, which is the reason he was there in the first place. (I was probably a little obnoxious, yelling at a priest again, but you do what you do.) After 15 minutes of arguing back and forth over this, James's protests suddenly stopped. He simply said, "I-I... Okay. I think I see what you mean." Days later, he called to tell me how well the service went and how the family was so grateful for his presence. I think he knew there was a problem with his refusal to serve. He just didn't know what it was or what to do about it. Maybe that's why he called for my WWND? answer.

On another occasion, James came over to our house so clearly upset that Al and I allowed him to smoke in our kitchen, something we'd almost always banished him to the porch to do.

He shared with us how the new pastor at his parish refused to acknowledge his gestures of friendship and collaboration, literally shutting him out of work, and even out of a part of the rectory. Al and I shot wide-eyed glances at each other as we listened to the "disconnect" between what had happened and what James *thought* had happened between them. I had to explain as delicately as I could that this person was no friend; and that one broke my heart. James had been so sincere in his outreach to his colleague. I wanted to find that guy and smack him. But these conversations reminded me of our misunderstanding over his no-show when I was pregnant with Nic. James didn't mean to misunderstand a lot, he just did. He didn't intend to be misunderstood a lot. He just was.

And then there's Nic.

The sunny, cheery, innocent personality of someone with Down syndrome may be something of a stereotype, but it is definitely a large part of Nic's persona. No one, even a person with Down syndrome, is sunny, cheery, and innocent all the time, yet Al and I are continuously amazed by the response of people to the undefinable spark that is so much a part of Nic. Our challenge is his darker side in those moments when he seems to lack the skills he needs to be understood, and then lashes out. Social skills are not just about charm – the social skills for which we need to give Nic support are the skills he has to draw on when he's angry, when he's bored, when he doesn't want to go to the bathroom and he really, really should. How does he handle those moments? What skills does Nic lack? How can I help? Our challenge is not how to help, but how to help *consistently* to grow his skills and to help him maintain them in our home and everywhere they challenge us.

If social skills are that important, I find myself thinking how dementia, a brain injury, or depression really can change the landscape. I find myself wondering how to help someone navigate the world when they're social skills just aren't what they used to be. And I really find myself wondering how I can thicken my skin enough to not take what I hear too personally. And as for disability, if the social skills are lacking, how can I teach the value of the skills and help the person acquire what they need to cultivate relationships?

I suppose we who try to support our loved ones in difficult times need to develop a bit of a tougher hide in those sensitive moments following a hurtful action or remark. Perhaps we need to discern that what could hurt us may not be about hurting us at all – it might just be a manifestation of someone else's struggle.

It's that whole Golden Rule thing – still so true. As a child, my mother's version of it was, "Do unto others as you would have them do unto you." What a thought to insert into unpleasant situations; the ones where I wanna pounce, the ones where I find myself losing control. My social skills matter too. Would I want Nic to treat me the way I treat him when I'm angry? And if I see him becoming aggressive or overly emotional, is it because of what I did *unto him*? In those moments of challenge for me, can I remember that it's *my* social skills that can make the difference between a bad moment and a really bad day?

Eat Something Together

"Wherefore, my brethren,
when ye come together to eat,
tarry for one another."
– 1 Corinthians 11:33

My husband, Al, is a very good cook. As much as knowing one's way around a kitchen is a survival tool for a man with a wife who works a lot of nights and who would also just as soon eat cold cereal at any meal, it is also a bit of a hobby and an art form in Al's eyes. I am not okay with receiving kitchen gadgets as gifts, but Al was quite pleased with the fancy-schmancy Wusthof bread knife that the kids gave him for Father's Day last year. When we have gatherings at our house, the guests do not compliment me on the delicious food, ever, even when I do bake, sauté, or roast. They just assume Al did the cooking, and well, really, they're usually right. I do not get to bask in the glow of the adulation of those whom I've served in my home because through the years, little by little, our friends, family, and I all realize that meals just taste better when Al makes them. It was how Al first got in good with my mother, actually. On our second Thanksgiving together before we married, Al volunteered to cook the turkey at my parents' house, and it is still his job 19 years later. As I write this, I'm thinking that the abdication of the cooking thing may be inherited – even my grandmother had a cook. Mothers often have enough stuff to do anyway, right? But I still maintain, mostly verbally and with precious little proof, that I am, or can be when given a chance, a fairly good cook.

Though I get no enjoyment from praise over the preparation and presentation of the meal, what I do get to enjoy is the part about sitting down and sharing food with friends. It was something I used to do with James before our parting of the ways, long before his accident. It was how we got to know each other. When I was working on my doctorate, I would often start my Saturday by going to James's parish for 7:00 AM mass, after which he would make Pop Tarts with melted butter that carbed me up for a long day of dissertation writing at the university. He and I often grabbed lunch at Bennigan's for some reason, and Bennigan's, like eating out with James, is now pretty much a thing of the past. The Bennigan's we used to go to was converted into a diner, a shiny, loud place that doesn't serve the deep-friend appetizers we like to dip in marinara sauce. It is just not the same.

I often bring James some kind of carby junk food when I visit the nursing home – chips, cookies, whatever. And I didn't stop when I found out he was on a diet of pureed food. I hadn't been told, and he hadn't choked, so I continued to bring tasty bad stuff and hope for the best. But sometimes when bringing food, it felt too much like feeding my daughters' guinea pigs in their cage, putting in a carrot – well, in this case, a cookie – and watching it be snatched away and rapidly devoured with nothing but the sound of chewing, kind of unsatisfying, one sided, not at all what eating together once was or is supposed to be. Sometimes James would offer me a piece of what he was eating, but I would most often say no. After all, he was always, like, ravenously hungry and living on beige food, so how could I take the fun munchies away from him?

But, hey, sometimes I was pretty hungry too. Stopping by after teaching an evening class, I was usually more than ready for a meal! I started thinking about one of our mutual favorites, pizza. There's a little shop a block down the hill from the nursing home, and the phone number on their sign is too big to miss, so one night, hungry as we both were for some real food, I called the pizza place from James's room, then walked down the block in the rain to pick up a small thin-crust pie.

Perhaps the nursing home staff turned a blind eye and blind nose to the heavenly aroma as I stealthily yet obviously slipped a small, plain pie through the hallway to James's room. Perhaps the aides made a mental note about the marinara-scented woman who would probably create a choking hazard in room 458, and they compassionately looked the other way. Pizza Claus made her first of many visits that night, and she seemed a most welcome sight from where James lay in his bed.

Lying in bed eating pizza? It wasn't Bennigan's and would probably lead to indigestion for the poor guy, but it wasn't nursing home food either. And it wasn't me watching someone else eat. It was two old friends having a meal together, as we did so many times when life was different seven years before.

"Oh, this is so damn good," he said of the pizza one night. I agreed. *This* was so damn good.

My mother really doesn't cook anymore. It was never Nola's favorite aspect of homemaking anyway. Unfortunately, when she gets depressed, she stops eating too. This leaves my father, a man of a generation accustomed to being waited on, to fend for himself, a task he does not do willingly or as healthfully as he should. Over the last few months, my brother Mike and sister Gail and I became aware of the problem and began to cook our parents' dinners for them. Spooning meat, starch, and veggies into Styrofoam containers we marked with the contents and the date, we made our best first efforts at ensuring that they were getting at least one full meal a day. Each of us takes a week (Al usually takes mine) and we cycle through, sibling by sibling. Mike, Gail, and I make 12 containers for the week, so our parents have six days' worth of food, but we do not make a meal for the seventh day. On the seventh day, we try to eat together as a family.

Sometimes our crew goes to the diner with the killer deserts in Vincentown or to my father's beloved Chinese buffet for all the shrimp he can pile on a dinner plate. Sometimes we order in and eat off paper plates. We sit down at Lloyd and Nola's dining table or perhaps in a restaurant, but we sit down together and share a meal, as we did on so many occasions when life was different. It's social. It's mutual – it's more than the food. It's the sharing of a pleasant and nourishing experience for body and soul. I think that eating together has more to it than just satisfying hunger. I'm a believer in all that research about families being happier when they eat together regularly. Even when it's out of a carton, eating together is about sharing, learning from one another, and experiencing comfort, all while the shrimp lo mein is getting passed around the table. It's about nurturing people, about being creative, uh, well, on Al's part, mostly – just so much more than filling the belly.

Any part of that definition sounds so damn good, I think.

Support Haircuts, Manicures, and Spiffing Up

"You look mahvelous."
– Billy Crystal

For much of my life my mother has instructed my siblings and me that when the day comes that she is laid out in her coffin and getting ready to meet her maker, we need to be sure her eyebrows are penciled in properly and that her hair looks perfect. This is not exactly a joke. She once threatened to sit up in her coffin and open one eye at me if I failed to attend to her appearance. I was too young at the time to know whether or not she was kidding. I even know which cosmetics to shop for; Nola's choice has always been a Maybelline brown eyebrow pencil, the little red one with the red cap. And as for the hair, I'll give the cosmetician photos. A bottle of Roux Fanci-Full in Sparkling Silver and perhaps carry a comb in my pocket to her funeral, just in case the bangs aren't sitting just right.

But enough of that – way too creepy.

Since Nola is still quite alive, I can tell you that the hair and eyebrow issue continues to be of great importance to my mother. Throughout my childhood, a trip to the hairdresser was a bi-weekly ritual for Nola, the one bit of essential personal indulgence that she never neglected. After leaving the Bronx in 1997 for the "active adult" community where my parents now reside, one of Nola's first quests was to find a hairdresser who could do her hair the way she wanted it, a person who possessed the skill and the savvy to understand just how important it was that the hair be cut just right, that its natural crazy curliness be downplayed, and that it be completely and utterly weatherproof. In between salon visits, I am sometimes called upon to be my mother's fill-in barber, for a "little shaping". I position her on the hamper in her bathroom (since it's high enough and backless) and I give her just that. She says she's not herself if the hair is not right. All is well in Nola's world if she is *not* talking about her hair and if the eyebrows are penciled in, nice and medium brown.

. . .

When I saw James for the first time after all those years it looked like he hadn't had a real haircut in months. I found this disheveled look quite distracting on a man who had always been very meticulous about his appearance. I noticed early on that James had an odd way of wearing his sideburns – he didn't wear sideburns at all. He kept them completely non-existent, shaved back to above his ears, perhaps some leftover from being in the Navy, maybe just a quirk, but when I found him they were so *there*. I wondered if it might lift his spirits to pay a little attention to his appearance now that his medical issues had stabilized. So about three weeks later I offered to bring my "barber kit", the very one I use on Nola, and cut his hair, sideburns and all. My makeshift barbershop would be located in the sitting room of the nursing home since his bedroom was too small and dark, and he was okay with this very public placement.

"Who is this lady cutting your hair, Father?", asked a gentleman sitting nearby one day.

"My best friend," James replied.

. . .

I remember visiting my godmother, Mabel, years ago in the nursing home where she lived during the last years of her life. She would often ask me to brush her hair because it felt so good. Me, I hate people touching my head at all, but this simple act gave her pleasure, so I did it for her whenever she asked. Often, when I stopped by, I would notice how pretty her hands looked. It turned out that her daughter-in-law came by and gave her a manicure every week. My godmother probably never went much further than the chapel in the nursing home, but she always looked good doing it. Hopefully, coiffed and polished, she felt better as well.

"Support haircuts, manicures, and general spiffing up" – I think that would make a cool bumper sticker. Sometimes it's a question of finding a way to give someone a visible measure of the way they were when they were at their best, like Nola, James, and my godmother. Sometimes it's about helping someone be a better version of who they are right now, perhaps a little more comfortable with the image they present to the world at this point in their lives. I think looking good helps you feel good too, even if you aren't going anywhere in particular.

Perhaps there's something about who spiffs you up that matters, too. Although my mother and dad paid my way through parochial school, piano lessons, and NYU, and despite the academic initials after my name, my role as personal beautician to Nola, this relatively recent sideline of mine, is one of my skills that she feels good about in an immediate and personal way. I've given James haircuts about every three weeks since that first trim in our makeshift sitting room barbershop. We even found a more private location when he was moved to a larger room. I think he and his family have come to expect that I'll take care of that small aspect of his personal care, and that's fine with me.

These people, they trust me with how they present themselves to the world.

They trust me using scissors close to their heads.

I must not disappoint.

I must not draw blood.

Incidentally, I used to cut Nic's hair but, he's a big kid now, and going to the barber has become a ritual to do every six weeks with his dad. At 12, he is all about cologne (a little too much cologne) and wearing a tie whenever possible. He is probably the only sixth grader in the school wearing a tie, but Nic has never been afraid of making the occasional bold fashion statement.

Distract!

*"A good advertisement is one which
sells the product without drawing
attention to itself."*
– David M. Ogilvy

Because I don't always have a great behavioral strategy for bringing heated moments with Nic down to a reliably calmer level, I have a cheesy but reliable alternative: I make him laugh. Sometimes the best thing to do about what's happening with Nic is to make something better happen before circumstances deteriorate any further. Taking advantage of his sense of humor to diffuse a potentially tense situation works almost all the time, plus I love making Nic laugh. I've also got a few other tools:

"Let's call Aunt Gail (Granola / Uncle Mike / insert name here)!"

"Can you help me with this?"

"Ah, go shoot some hoops, boy."

"Let's bake cookies!"

"Are you looking at me?" using a DeNiro *Taxi Driver* voice, two fingers pointing to me, then turning to him.

"Uh, hey man, where's the love?" which may generate a hug; as well as assorted songs, tangos, or two-person conga lines.

After a successful experience with distracting Nic into a better mood, I'm always surprised by how well diverting someone's attention can work to get difficult situations back on track. Distraction is one of those standard-issue behavioral strategies you might see on a children's behavior plan for redirecting conduct, Nic's plan included. The strategy a parent chooses is ideally based on their understanding of what sets the behavior in motion and whether the usual consequence for that behavior is somehow rewarding to the child. Even getting yelled at is a reward for certain children. Attention is attention for some. Negative or positive, they're not picky. (I learned this at 23 from one of my sixth-grade students back in the Bronx. Thanks, Jason, wherever you are.)

Based on what I know about Nic's behavior, I could also physically remove him from what's going on. I could simply correct him and tell him what he should do. Or with that, you know, 20/20 hindsight I get after my large-scale parenting mistakes, I can make sure that he's got enough structure and predictability in the situation so that he doesn't *need* to lose control (after all, he's communicating something) and have to be distracted from what he's about to do that is going to get him in trouble.

But when I think about it, distraction works for me too. Distracting myself can be as simple as turning on the radio and getting lost in some good tunes or cranking up the comedy channel in the car for a laugh instead of thinking the sad thoughts on yet another long ride to work; or perhaps making a phone call when I start to feel like I've been alone in the house too long. Distraction lightens my mood, even if it's just for a while, helps me step away from what's bugging me, and helps me get a little perspective; for as Nola likes to say, "This too shall pass." I wish it would pass before one of my other distractions, (AKA eating everything carby I can find) kicks in.

When it comes to managing Nic's outbursts, it's good to realize that sometimes he and I can turn back, sometimes we can start over. But for those times when we can't do anything besides be in this difficult moment, a diversion, preferably a pleasant diversion, may be in order. It's all about getting to a better place, even if it's just for a while. Not just for Nic, but for me too.

To Be Honest, I Get Something Out Of This, Too

"Love is love's reward."
– John Dryden

Every now and then as we sit together in Room 458, James just looks over at me and says, "Thank you." When there's not a snack in my hand for him, this takes me by surprise. I generally do not respond, "You're welcome" to his unexpected words of appreciation because I don't usually understand why he's saying it when I hear it. Dense as I can sometimes be, I will cock my head and say, "Thank you for what?" and he'll respond with something to the effect of, "For all the little things you do." And with a reply like that, he pretty much buys himself the probability of many more little things.

The other day, as we were hanging around doing nothing, James asked, "Why do you bother with me?" I think he knows how difficult he can be physically and emotionally on those who love him, maybe not in the moment, but it does seem to occur to him at various points. I'm truly awkward with the mushy response stuff, but I bother, of course, because I care.

My answer to, "Why do you bother?" however, was, "For the big check and the movie rights." Smooth, huh? Fortunately, he got it.

The second time James asked me why I bothered, we were in the same place doing the same nothing, but the mood was different and I knew it. I found him in the hallway that afternoon, sitting in the long line of residents facing the nurse's station dozing in their wheelchairs.

I whisked James back to his room and sunk into the wingchair across from him. We just sat there, silent and sad. The gravity of his situation, in those moments, is inescapable. You can almost feel prison bars around him. That time, when he asked me why I bother, I gave him a big dose of mushy stuff.

My friend Kate has heard many of my James, Nic and Nola stories. God bless her ears. When she hears the James story, she generally replies, "You're a saint, Ger." An overstatement for sure, but that's what friends are for, so thank you, Kate.

Obviously, I don't show up for the movie rights, there is no big check, and I am a bit intimidated by even a casual association to the unreachable goodness that merits the title *saint*. I show up just because it galls me to no end that someone so relatively young has been left to live his life out in a nursing home. I show up maybe because I have some resources and knowledge of the "system", thanks to my husband's experience as a social worker. I show up with a flickering sense of awe because I remember the strange persistent voice insisting that I find James after seven years of minimal contact, and my shock at what I found. I show up most certainly because I love my *Dear*, my curly-haired pretty-eyed, honey-voiced, brother from another mother. But mostly I "bother" to show up because, perhaps selfishly, it makes me feel good to do it.

I don't have to show up with my rotation of weekly dinners for my mother anymore; we've hired help now. It's a two-hour round-trip to visit my parents, so a visit of any substance usually consumes the full day. Sometimes when we arrive, I slip into their house first and leave the kids and Al in the living room with my father while I talk Nola out of her bed and the funk I often find her in. Sometimes, to my great joy and relief, she greets us at the front door, overjoyed to see the grandchildren and that swarthy couple who drove them to her house. There are easier ways to spend a Sunday, but going to my parents' house puts my mind at rest for the coming week. Al and I do a quick med check, peek into the refrigerator to see if there's enough food to last until the housekeeper returns to cook, then open up the conversation about where we're having dinner tonight. In the end, I'm always glad my little crew and I showed up.

. . .

We may never receive the thanks we think we deserve, or that we truly deserve, for the good things we do. Like, sometimes I make some gesture that I think is the good deed of the century, and no one says a word. Other times, I don't even realize what it is that I've done that someone is so grateful for. I guess the only thing we can be sure of is the reasons we choose to do good. It may become the difference between continuing what we're doing and stopping cold without looking back. I've come to believe that the best reason to do what I do is because it feels right, that it somehow fills a need that I have in myself. In that sense, maybe it's not such a big sacrifice, but more of a choice. Maybe we do for others because we *want* to do for others, not because of how they will respond. I hope that what I do is truly good for the person for whom I do it, like my parents or James, but I can only hope. I do what I do because it feels right to do it and really, that's all I can be sure of anyway.

Loneliness is the Biggest Disability

*"The most terrible poverty is loneliness,
and the feeling of being unloved."*
– Mother Theresa

My father, Lloyd, brought his new bride to New York City from their native Jamaica in 1960. He had lived on the upper west side of Manhattan for several years, but met my mother when he was back visiting the West Indies in the late 50s. After their brief courtship, my mother said goodbye to her family in Jamaica and became part of her new husband's family, since many of them had already left the island for New York City. Beach-loving Nola told me she'd once joked to some of her friends that the only reason she'd move to New York City would be because she lost her mind, or because she was madly in love. I'm hoping she came because of the latter.

My parents' first years together always sounded cramped and crazy, but a little fun, too. Nola and Lloyd lived in a three-family house where his cousin, Russel, his wife, and his wife's parents lived. My mother and my father's cousin's wife, my Aunt Olga, became the best of friends. And they still are, although many miles separate them now. My father and his cousin worked for their family business polishing brass and steel exteriors of some of New York City's most famous buildings. It was Aunt Olga's mother, my "Grandma White", who first called me Gerry when I was a baby because she thought Geralyn was too long of a name for an infant, and I've been called Gerry ever since. There were other friends from Jamaica not too far away, like the people who would become me and my sister's godparents, and even Colin Powell's parents were acquaintances (I had to slip that in there, because the general and I have the same godmother). My father's two brothers and his sister started life in America in the New York City area, too. Our small family was peppered all over the five boroughs.

Nola and Lloyd bought a house of their own in the Bronx in 1964, the one I knew as my childhood home. They lived in our three bedroom brick "pre-war", with a shared driveway for almost 35 years. Other relatives and friends slowly fanned out a little more into the more affluent suburbs, but we could find them all within an hour's commute. Our family gathered together often, and uncles and aunts were not averse to dropping in unexpectedly. Although I recall one photograph of my mother covering her face with her hands because relatives popped in when – God forbid – her hair was in curlers. I think, on the whole, they had a pretty good time together. I remember Calypso, savory foods, and a good bit of rum punch being poured on our back porch in the summers. Although my mother missed her family terribly, her culture was all around her in the little enclave into which she married. Nola would eventually widen her circle of friends on her own, through the friendships she made with other young mothers on our street, through her job in a local thrift shop, and with the mothers of my friends and Gail's. Nola never seemed to have any trouble making and keeping friends, and when my parents moved to New Jersey, it was just more of the same for her. If Nola was ever lonely, it was not because she didn't know how to draw people in.

· · ·

For Nic, friendship has had its obstacles, some created by his physical and developmental challenges. By comparison to his sister Courtney, I often feel I failed him; but then his sister navigated the social world effortlessly, even as a toddler. I remember my daughter at three, introducing me to some girls she was playing with by saying, "This is my friend, Mommy," and entering preschool classes by shouting, "Hi everyone, I'm here!" Even today, the most I have to do to help her socially is to make sure I pay the phone bill and fill my gas tank.

Like his sister, Nic is really sociable, too. He, too, will burst into a room with a big hello, but the phone calls don't come fast and furious like they do with Courtney. Part of me guesses that there's a gender difference here, too, but since I've only got one child of each gender, there's no one else with whom to compare them. Part of me guesses that even though Nic was included in typical classrooms for several years, his verbal communication and learning issues sometimes separated him in too large of a way from his typical peers, and might have made some parents a little nervous about having him over for a play date. Part of me also knows that I don't always step up as well as I should about play dates too, because it's a lot of work, and I didn't have to do it with Courtney, and because often the invitation isn't reciprocated, and I get a little resentful of that sometimes. I'm still working on this, by the way, but you know that.

Realizing Nic's social challenges in elementary school, our educational team developed a "Circle of Friends" for Nic during third and fourth grades. This idea was something I'd read about as an empowering process for people with disabilities, or anyone who is experiencing challenges in making and keeping friends (It's sometimes called "a Circle of Support" for adults). A colleague and I presented on creating circles to local parent groups, and Nic's team all saw its value for him once we shared it with them, too. Originating in Canada, Jack Pierpoint, Marsha Forest, and Judith Snow called them circles because of the idea that we all have "circles" of friends, acquaintances, and other people with various levels of closeness in our lives. To explain the concept in presentations, my colleague and I would have participants draw four concentric circles and fill them in with names. In the center they would write the names of family and people who were like family to them. In the second circle, they'd fill in names with close friends, and the third, acquaintances, and in the fourth, people they pay to be in their lives such as an aide, a teacher, a doctor, even a hairstylist – someone who would not be there for free. The point of the exercise was to show that individuals with disabilities often have too many people in the paid section, and not enough in the second and third circles where friends and acquaintances go. (Too often, you see these disparities very plainly once you draw the circles and write in the names.) The object of creating the Circle of Friends for someone is to help them start the process of filling in those empty spaces with real relationships through a creative, ongoing commitment to the process that lies ahead.

This Circle at school was comprised of Nic and several children in his grade who were interested in getting together socially once a week for about an hour with an adult supervising them. The group would do a project together, have a snack, perhaps play a game. All the while talking about some aspect of friendship. I loved the times when Nic brought home the artwork they created together in their circle, and he always proudly hung their work on his bedroom wall. The part I liked even better was that the other children in the group benefited too. Since they all got to hang out, they all worked together to create collages and murals about the topics they chose, and they all got to learn about friendship, not just Nic. They also got a chance to be with each other in the room, all around the school, and in the community. It did, indeed, widen Nic's circle, and it gave each child in the group at least one new friend in their lives, too.

· · ·

My mother has never lost her ability to make and be a friend to others, and the fact that she is this way has always carried her through tough times. Nola is a note-writer, a regular phone-caller, a visitor. And even an emailer at age 82. Her life, as I've seen it, has provided her with the generous return of those connections from family and friends. What is most alarming and disturbing to me about the phases when she takes to her bed for days is that this choice to withdraw takes Nola so far from the company of others, the very atmosphere in which she shines the brightest. I wish that my mother could see as clearly as my father and siblings and I do, the transformation that occurs when she makes the effort to join the party in those difficult moments. She always succeeds. Nola's outgoing nature is still there to carry her through; she just needs to give herself a push. But I don't think that is as easy as it sounds these days.

Although it is more of an effort for Nic to maintain the connections he makes, those connections are an important part of the success of his life. Though Nola and Nic have their challenges, the biggest challenge – the biggest disability that each of them or any of us could face, in my opinion – is isolation and loneliness. I think that you do not have to be brilliant in this life; you have to be connected to other people, even if it's only just a few solid gems you know are always gonna be there for you. Sometimes you need help with making connections, and sometimes you don't. If you do, as Nic sometimes does, it's a question of bringing in support in the form of a mother who will step up and make phone calls he can't easily make; in the form of bringing in other adults and peers who know him in settings like school to help make a plan; and in the form of keeping the social effort going when it's just as easy and so much less risky to slack off. I'm working on this, too. (WWND?)

· · ·

As I visit the nursing home week after week, I am sobered by the loneliness that pervades the place despite available activities and well-meaning staff and volunteers. I say hello to the people I pass in a line of wheelchairs in the hallways, if they're awake. James is in that line all too often. My greetings seem like so little; I don't even know all their names. Even the most well-meaning nurse, aide or volunteer, cannot replace family and friends and home. I think of the basic idea behind Nic's Circle, that the people who are paid to be in your life should not outnumber everyone else. I see greeting cards on James's dresser sometimes when I visit, sometimes from the same senders again and again, sometimes an outpouring of greetings for special occasions like his birthday or Christmas. His mother and his brother Joe are there daily. James's other siblings visit, too. His best friend Bob, from childhood, visits every week. And there's me. Is that enough? Is loneliness James's biggest disability?

Advocating for Someone Else is Tricky Business

"It's time to go to the mattresses."
– The Godfather

Easily fifteen years ago, a woman I worked with said to me in conversation that I was a nice person, but that she wouldn't mess with me. I thought this was about the coolest thing anyone ever said about me to my face. I grew up following the rules more often than not and saying "yes" when I was expected to and "no" when I was expected to – out of respect, out of expectation, maybe even out of fear. As an adult, I remember watching the movie *Zelig* with my husband and his friend, and feeling a little uncomfortable that I was identifying with the main character even while I was laughing at him. I sometimes felt I was too much like a Leonard Zelig even before I saw the movie. Woody Allen's Zelig had the "remarkable" ability to become just like whatever or whoever he was near, to the extent that he could even resemble them physically. A human chameleon; not a flattering comparison to make to myself, eh? I often feel that I try too hard to do what is expected of me rather than what I feel like doing, especially when I was younger. My coworker's comment made me feel as though perhaps I *did* have some chops after all, maybe even a bit of an edge – wow – and that someone had picked up on it. Perhaps I was starting to be a little less Zelig at last.

Still, I dread speaking in front of colleagues at faculty meetings, nice as they are, even after 10 years at the university. I can't believe I have a job which requires me to speak authoritatively for a living. Little black clouds form around my head and I automatically avert my eyes when I deal with people with whom I am uncomfortable. I wish I could force my disdain to either vanish or intimidate the hell out of other people, but no luck so far. My children have learned to say "You decide" when there's a decision to be made because they hear me say it way too often. People tend to think I'm easy-going, when the truth may be that really I am sometimes a five-foot, eight-inch wild-haired wimp.

Surprisingly, though, it seems that I am the least Zelig when I have to speak for someone else. I did hone my edge here and there through the years, standing up to various people and surviving it, thus leading me to stand up to a few more people and survive that, too. I've even learned that you can disagree with real friends and still be friends.

Yes! True! Who knew?

It has taken time and the repetition of the same experiences again and again for me to finally acquire the ability to be assertive, but I really honed my edge after having Nic. I think my very last moments of full-time Zelig were with the pediatrician who dismissed my questions about the strange upper body movements Nic was making as an infant. You remember that she told me what I had hoped to hear; that the ticks would pass, that they were just a leftover reflex. But they did not pass. The ticks got worse and worse. I will probably never forgive myself for not videotaping those moments – the earliest and most damaging of his seizures – and then tying her to a chair 'til she looked at them, saw exactly what I was talking about, and advised me what to do about it. Too Zelig, too long. Why didn't I question? Why wasn't I a better advocate for this baby who was in so much trouble?

It's a question I continue to try to answer for myself. I will never be able to go back and fix the decision to go along, to stick with the first, quite uninformed answer I was given and leave it at that. I am trying to question more and trying to advocate more immediately, but it's still a struggle for me. I want to be nice! I want you to like me! I want everybody to be happy! I want authorities to have the answers. And I give them lots, perhaps too much, rope and hope they don't hang themselves and me – yet sometimes they do.

Oh wait, but I want what I want, too. In this particular case, I want the best for my child, well, both children actually.

Wouldn't it be great if I could be nice and get what I want? Wouldn't it be great if I could advocate the best for my children without making enemies along the way? What I really want is for my friend's words to be true: *Heh, nice person, but don't mess with her*, to which I'd add, *do not mistake her mild manner for weakness.* The quote, "Nothing is as strong as gentleness and nothing is so gentle as real strength" is this woman's mantra now. Go, me!

. . .

Hospitals and schools became my first practice at advocating for someone else. I learned to question *everything* doctors said after Nic's disastrous seizures, because I finally realized, perhaps too late in some ways, that even the best doctors simply don't always have the answer. To this day, I retain great respect for Nic's neurologist whose answer to my question, "Why won't the seizures stop?" was an honest, "I don't know." Sometimes family and physician have to find the answers together. Not a bad thing, this collaboration. It's a give and take because we both have knowledge that the other needs to better define and solve problems. I try to be calm in my newfound assertiveness, because the first time I had a what-would-Nola-do-moment of commanding the situation and people listened to me, I felt like I'd acquired superpowers. My wrath once rattled the windows in the intensive care unit when an attending physician, a man who treated Nic one time too many for his taste, informed me quite casually that, mm, the next time Nic got sick, I should take him to a different hospital. Fortunately, this unleashing of pent-up frustration became more the exception than the rule. And even more fortunately, that particular doctor became a radiologist.

Back to collaboration.

From preschool up to five minutes ago, Nic's education has been an adventure in advocacy for Al and me. I believe, as a former elementary school teacher, that most educators really are doing their best with what they have and what they know from the systems to which they have access. We come together to talk about a child using different data; mine from home, the teachers' from the school day. We find commonalities and differences. We try to listen to each other, but sometimes we do not agree. The teacher considers decisions as they affect the child's school year. The child's family considers decisions as they impact his entire life. Parents think 18-to-life, cradle-to-grave, womb to tomb, birth to earth. But sometimes, our different perspectives dovetail, and sometimes there is friction.

Advocating for someone else is tricky business. To Merriam-Webster, the word *advocate* means to plead the cause of another. Advocating is what Al and I do when we sit down with the teachers and therapists on Nic's educational team. Advocating is what I do when I get on the phone with my parents' long-term care insurance company and ask for more in-home services for my mother. Advocating is what I tried to accomplish by writing an impassioned letter to James's employer, the Archdiocese, to transition him out of the nursing home to a more appropriate setting. So far, I have met with mixed success in these three arenas. I am a woman ever in search of advice on advocacy. I am a woman in an ongoing state of chops development.

What do I need to bring to the advocacy table or to the letter I'm whacking out on the laptop on behalf of my son, my mother, or my friend? In search of an answer to keep me from sounding like the clacking wheels on some emotional rollercoaster, I pulled a veteran advocate acquaintance – and fellow parent – named Ruth Landsman out of a meeting we were attending with a promise of a quick question and a cup of coffee. She gave me a lot. She gave me so much more. "You have to know the rules of the system," she said. "All an advocate has is their credibility. If you go in and you are asking for something that is not required, something that is pie-in-the-sky, you lose that credibility. You lose your power, because they can legitimately say, 'Hell no'." Maybe that's why meetings of any sort can really work my nerves. Sometimes, it feels like every word I utter carries so much weight.

And Ruth continued, "You have to learn the rules in the system. The people you are dealing with are offering you, in most cases, what they have available. In my professional life, I know how easy it is to say, 'I've got A and B. Will either of these help you?,' versus, 'What is it you need that I might have to go out on a hunt for?'"

Familiarity with special education laws through my roles as teacher and professor has helped me to advocate for Nic, no doubt. I can wade through the sea of acronyms and jargon that can muddy the waters of understanding in special education. I have a husband who never misses a meeting, so we're always together. I'm never alone. I know what an "observable measurable objective" is supposed to look like. Strange, though, that when my students say to me, "It must be so much easier for you to advocate since you know the law," I still tell them, "Yes, but no, no, no!" It's easier, yes, because I have some information, but more difficult because I teach the ideal and we are sometimes so far from the ideal in real life. What's most difficult is that I am speaking on behalf of someone I love and will worry about for the rest of my life. This is not theory for me when we sit down to talk about Nic. I am his *mommy*.

"The role of the advocate is to stop the professional before they get to the 'but,'" Ruth continued, "because what comes after the 'but' is not good news."

I've heard the "but" with Nic, with my mother, and with James. It sounds like this:

"Nic's a great kid, but..."

"Your mother demonstrates some need, but..."

"This is not the ideal place for a man James's age, but..."

So what do I do with all these *buts*? I think I ought to try to do my homework, and a lot of listening, and a lot of observing, and thinking about and respecting the needs and wishes of the person for whom I advocate, as well as the perspective of those on the other side of the table. I need to deeply know the needs and the wishes of Nic, Nola, or James, call them by concrete, understandable, achievable names. My wishes and dreams can't be more important to the conversation than theirs. I need to be creative and clear before the other side can slip in a "but." And I need to be open to possibilities we have not entertained, because somewhere between what Al and I want and what they want to give, there's something that's going to work, if only on the way to the next time we sit at the table.

Is there a second to take a breath and pray for help and clarity here, too?

There'd better be.

Part 4 – Disability

Don't Talk About People Like They Aren't There

"Don't talk about people like they aren't there. What you are is a question only you can answer."
– Lois McMaster Bujold

I don't think I immediately noticed that I was speaking for Nic. With a baby or a toddler, people seem to naturally ask the nearest relevant grownup what the child wants to eat, to do, all that. And that's how it started, normally enough. But Nic grew older and his speech intelligibility did not keep pace; he often sounds like a very large toddler, using short phrases instead of detailed sentences, using a select few sounds in place of the more refined articulation children typically develop over time. Seeing evidence of Down syndrome on his face, perhaps some people just thought he couldn't answer or that he did not understand the question. Sometimes, after hearing an unintelligible answer, I would quickly chime in with a translation, until I all but stopped bothering to give Nic the space to try to answer for himself at all. Was that from my own embarrassment or for me to speed the process, or what? More and more, I seemed to become my son's interpreter, intentionally or not. When Nic hit school age and the kids on the playground after school started to ask me the questions they'd normally ask Nic, I realized that it was my place to do some redirecting of them as well as myself.

"What's his name?" says one kid.

"Well, why don't you ask him?" I say, stopping myself from answering. And often, they will ask.

"How old is he?" asks another kid.

"How old are you, Nic?" I ask, and I wait for his answer. If he says the wrong number, I may correct him, if it matters. Uh, or if it's not too far off, who cares?

This talking to a person with a disability through another person, I found, was not a response to one particular type of disability or something only children do. When visiting the nursing home late in the evening, I have several times been asked if I wanted James to sit in his wheelchair or if I would prefer that he lie in his bed during our visit. *Wait, you're asking me?*

It's one of those responses I find myself aware of in myself and others, this tendency to make decisions or speak in the place of another who is assumed unable to communicate their own choices. Answering for someone may expedite the conversation for one who either can't answer fast enough or isn't assumed to be able to answer correctly or at all – but how can that always be okay? It runs the danger of trivializing the person to the point of invisibility.

I hereby vow to only answer for Nic or James if they don't understand the language of the person doing the asking but I do. And so far, no one who only speaks Spanish has made any request of either of them, in front of me. So thank God, 'cause my Spanish is not that great. But, you know, you get my point.

You are More than the Name for What You Have

*"It is in the knowledge of the genuine
conditions of our lives that we must draw our
strengths to live and our reasons for living."*
– Simone de Beauvoir

James tells me he's *brain damaged*. I respond that he has a *brain injury*. Can you hear a difference? I hear two differences, which is why I try to use the second term to refer to his condition. As a person immersed in special education, as a parent of a child with a disability, a former special education teacher, as a professor of special education (I wasn't kidding about being immersed), I've picked up a few concepts that I think go beyond education and link into life in general. This one is about perception. How do you see yourself? Damaged. How do you describe yourself? Damaged? How does the choice of your words affect how others see you? Damaged.

My son, Nic, *has* Down syndrome. That's how I say it. I've heard it said that way by many parents I know who have kids with disabilities, not "*disabled*" kids. Nic *has* Down syndrome. But depending on who you ask, Nic is also mentally retarded, a "Downs child", a retarded child, a disabled child, and – *ewwww!* – a special child. There are lots of identifiers that place disability before his basic personhood and I hate them all. I don't think my disdain is denial; I just wish people who use terms like these would remember that he is a child first. He is more like other children than not, but he often gets singled out, in life and in the choice of descriptors used about him. So, I like to put the commonality first, *a child*, and the descriptor second, "*with* Down syndrome." In my world, they call it "person-first language."

Rosa's Law passed in 2010, and I'm looking forward to the eventual disassociation of the term *retarded* and its half-brother, *retard*, from people with intellectual disabilities. The family of a little girl named Rosa Marcelino, who has Down syndrome, took their offense at the term *retarded*, all the way to the Supreme Court. Perhaps the association of *retarded* and *retard* with people such as Nic will soon wither away; but if not, may they dissolve into the vernacular without future generations knowing where they began. I learned long ago that the man for whom Down syndrome was named, John Langdon Down, originally described the children he observed as having common facial features (distinct from other children with intellectual disabilities). He described them as *mongoloids*. Someone with Nic's disabilities was once referred to as a *mongoloid idiot*. We don't use these inaccurate terms anymore, but we still say *idiot*, you know? Since I learned its genesis, I try my best not to, but *idiot* is just now another insult and I'm guessing relatively few of us know its origin. I used it for a long time before I found out – and I feel guilty when it slips out of my mouth, even now.

Sometimes the idea of James saying "I'm brain damaged," stops me in my tracks more than his actual traumatic brain injury does. It makes him sound like he's the very different person I insist he's not. What must it feel like for James to describe himself that way? When I think of damage, I imagine the damaged goods section of the supermarket where the soup is cheaper because the can has a dent or the clothes pin bag has a hole in it that the store taped up and they took off 20%. Damage is something that happens to objects. It makes them less valuable.

Items get damaged, people get injured. Damaged stays damaged, but you can recover from an injury. I like the idea of James recovering from a brain injury and I'm sure he could develop an infinity for this idea as well, if he can just give it a chance.

Injury suggests a capacity for healing as well. It seems to me that two things are going on: One, you have an illness or a disability. Two, you have how you feel about your illness and disability. You may never recover from an illness, but how you feel about your illness, that can heal. You can heal from an injury, even if it's never cured. How great would it be if James could be healed of the feelings he has about his injury, whether or not he ever recovers from the brain injury itself?

How much peace would it bring to my mother to experience a healing of her depression because of what's happening to her?

. . .

Sometimes person-first language is a mouthful. I make my sentences longer but my intention clearer when I talk about my son who has an intellectual disability rather than my intellectually disabled son; but I do my best to try to use it when speaking about this particular attribute of Nic. It seems more respectful to me, making Down syndrome just another trait of Nic's, along with pre-teen, Pee-wee Herman video fan, Elvis aficionado, and reluctant church-goer. Person-first language makes brain injury an attribute of James', albeit, a major one. But it's another descriptor, along with priest, Irish guy, Dallas Cowboys fan, and lover of the pepperoni slice. It makes dementia a characteristic, not a full definition of my charming, caring, large-and-in-charge mother, Nola.

Language is powerful.

Make the Best Call

"The harder you fight to hold on to
specific assumptions,
the more likely there's gold in letting go of them."
– John Seely Brown

I get so frustrated with Nic sometimes. I get so frustrated *for* Nic all the time.

Frustrated *with* = "What are you saying, Nic?"

"I don't understand, Nic."

"Why are you doing that, Nic?"

"Nic, stop!"

Frustrated *for* = Nic's side, the flip side. "Why can't you understand me, Mom?"

"I think I'm gonna scream if you don't start gettin' what I'm sayin', Mom."

"Can't anybody understand me?"

"What's wrong with you guys?"

"I think I'm gonna hit somebody or hit myself in a minute here."

"Stop smiling and nodding. I know you don't have a clue."

And I'm his mother, taking an honest shot at trying to understand.

What about all those people out in the world who look at Nic's angelic face with its almond eyes and assume that he is "*special*," and that I am "*special*" because he is one of those "*special*" children that God only gives to "*special*" parents? (This almost always comes with a request that Nic give them a hug, a request often made in a tone of voice used to speak to toddlers.) How much time will they give to understanding his labored speech if they think he's so, so very "*special*" that regular expectations don't apply to him?

And how am I doing with that one myself?

Strangers don't generally request that James give them a hug. Thank God, in a way; how sad in another. James is much older now that he lives in a nursing home – not chronologically older, but old by association. Sitting dazed and bored at the nurses' station with the other residents doing the same idling until it's time for dinner. You can't tell that James is much younger than the octogenarian napping to his left. I am only 13 years younger than James, yet I am often asked if he is my uncle (if he's on the priest floor with the elderly retired clergy), or if I am his daughter (if we are in the basement by the vending machines where no one knows he's a priest). I can't tell you how much James hates hearing that second assumption. Oddly enough, little West Indian me has also been mistaken for his sister if we are seen in profile, but I digress.

The first assumption someone may make of a person who lives in a nursing home is that they are old, infirm, and incapable no matter what their age or whether they truly are. It comes with people talking to you in a louder voice and making sure you eat your vegetables like your mother did when you were a kid. And it seems to me that it's easy to not think twice about doing it.

Do first impressions count? I don't completely trust the impressions people make going on what they say when I first meet them. I try not to draw too much from how they look either, but that first moment in an encounter is a combination of intuition and a preconceived notion that's hard to completely disregard. I don't know if it's a distrust of letting that first feeling say it all or the need to take a little more than one meeting to feel that I can really trust what impresses me early in a relationship. I wrestle with the value of the first impression when I think of the Nics and Jameses of the world, the people who may be victim of more preconceived notion than intuition when someone sees them. What are we seeing in a person at first glance anyway? Is the way they look a reliable gauge?

Do they look the way they do because they are nervous?

Did they just hear some bad news?

Did they just lose a twenty?

It is much easier to think I can trust what I see when I look at someone for the first time, but that first glance is not so reliable either. It's been my experience that the later glances, especially those tempered with love and time, are much more trustworthy and somehow soften the edges enough to reveal the true person.

Case in point, I definitely have an extra sense called "Downdar". That's a word some people I know, and myself, use for the ability to scope out any person in the place with Down syndrome, whether you can see their facial features or not. Downdar is made up of recognizing the more compact body type, perhaps the walk, the relative smallness of the hand, or the sound of a voice that may struggle a bit with articulation. My friend, Claire, says it too often comes with stretch pants on women. What I see, what I hear, and what I feel when I see a person with Down syndrome has no doubt changed since I had Nicolas. Every stereotype of children with Down syndrome, those first impressions I'm supposed to get of a sweet, little elfin angel – did I get them before I had Nic? Was it a fair impression to get of other people with Down syndrome? I mean, how would you like it if you were a grown man or woman and people just immediately assumed you were a little elfin angel because you had Down syndrome?

Sometimes I wonder what people see instinctively in people like Nic, and what our biases and prejudices about disability do to our encounters with him and others who experience disability. Do we first see a person, then see what we *think* we are supposed to assume about someone like Nic before we respond? What do we do with this? The response is hard for us to even understand in ourselves. Do we truly comprehend how we make decisions and assumptions? Do we create stories to explain to ourselves what we know about Nic because we already have a story about Down syndrome in us? Do we create stories that explain the elderly person before us because we've already defined *elderly*? I probably do more often than I care to admit.

I want to value the second impression and the later glance along with the first one as reminders of the humanity and dignity not just of these people whom I love, but of people who may share the same challenges. It is a perspective I can always draw upon with some effort. I can't allow myself to only see stereotypes, but I will if I don't take the time, even if only a second or two, to identify what I'm seeing and assuming about you. It's all about taking the time. As I write this, I think that it may sometimes need to be a very deliberate effort at first.

I've heard this concept put a few ways in my life as a parent and as a teacher about people whose first impressions are complicated by the appearance of obvious disability. Anne Donnellan calls it "making the least dangerous assumption," Douglas Biklen says to "presume competence," and, similarly, William Stillman says to "presume intellect." Each of these quotes refers to people with significant challenges like intellectual disabilities and autism. But what if these declarations could be like a universal mantra, something to say or think at those moments when the temptation is to smile and nod, to look away, or to just go with the stereotype you harbor of the person before you and look no further?

I'm learning that I cannot assume anything about a person just by what I see, just by what I hear; It's not enough. It isn't fair. Without knowing for sure whether someone can do it, can understand it, can tell me it – whatever *it* is – I need to assume their competence and intellect, because I can't presume a lack of competence and intellect based only on what I see before me. If someone cannot do whatever *it* is, perhaps they lack the support they need to succeed. If someone cannot understand whatever *it* is, might it be because it has not been explained in a way that works for them? And if someone can't tell me it, can I help them find a way so that they can? It is safer to the person's welfare and more respectful of their dignity to indeed make the least dangerous assumption, the presumption of intellect, the presumption of competence. For in the words of Anne Donnellan, "Absence of evidence is not evidence of absence."

My little efforts at presuming intellect, by the way, often annoy James, Nicolas, and even Nola. Too many times for James's taste I have struck deals with him to get him from the nurses' station to his room.

"I'm tired. Could you wheel your chair to the third door? I'll push you the rest of the way."

Too many times for Nic's taste, I have refrained from my basic urge to do for Nic just to get on our way faster and have said, "You want to go out to eat, buddy? Then you need to go upstairs and get your hoodie. I'll be in the car."

And I have indeed dared to tell my mother, Nola, "I'll get the phone, but would you please order the Lo Mein since they know you at the take-out place?" And if she's in a good mood, I might add, "Your kids all know you can make a million phone calls when you want to."

I think it's sometimes easier to believe that we cannot or that we do not understand, and stop right there. It's easier to assume that we cannot do it – and that is the most dangerous assumption, especially if you have it of yourself.

Leave "Remember?" Off the End of the Sentence

"May I forget what ought to be forgotten, and recall, unfailing, all that ought to be recalled, each kindly thing, forgetting what might sting."
— Mary Carolyn Davies

My mother Nola always seemed to have control; control issues, maybe, self-control for sure. My first, worst example is that I can recall her having had absolutely no weight issues, even when I was a chunky teenager with a nasty sprinkle of forehead zits. My mother had only a ballpark idea of what she weighed at any given time. I bet she never even took her shoes off to get on a doctor's scale (I'll take my earrings off, my watch off if it buys me a couple of ounces). Nola would just say, "I need to cut down," if her pants started to feel tight, and off came that pesky five pounds.

Nola had pretty good control over other aspects of life too, which was quite evident to my sister and me. We grew up with early curfews, high standards, and a caveat, "Little children should be seen and not heard." Unlike our friends, Gail and I were never allowed to answer, "What?" or, "Yeah?" to her call, but strictly, "Yes, mom?" I still remember thinking I was such a rebel when I started taking "mom" off, and just answering, "Yes?" (I was probably off to college by then.)

In hindsight, I think in ignoring the missing "mom," she was just letting go a little since she was done with that particular rule. Nola did let go of some other rules as we grew older, but she was always the team captain.

Control looks a bit different on Nola now. It's less about controlling us, and more about not losing control of herself. Control comes in the form of asking the same question again and again when there's new information to digest. It comes in the form of a lot of double-checking of the facts.

"When is the doctor's appointment again?"

"Was that doctor's appointment canceled?"

"Which doctor is this again?"

"Why do I have to go to some damn doctor anyway?"

"I'm not going to any damn doctor."

Control looks like little notes Nola scribbles to herself on scraps of paper that wind up all over the house. It comes in the worried voice of one who just isn't sure anymore, and knows it, but wants to feel in control.

Sometimes I don't want to answer the phone when it rings for that fourth or fifth time in rapid succession because I know that Nola's will be the voice on the other end yet again. I know the question is the same one as in the last call. I know I already answered it three or four times. If I answer it again, I will get snippy. I am a bit tired these days, but too much of a wimp to get too snippy. But sometimes, in frustration, I'll repeat the answer and tack on the word "remember?" to the end of the statement, as in, "I told you, the doctor's appointment is Thursday, remember?"

Well she may remember, but possibly she does not, for whatever reason. Why am I even asking? It is starting to seem to me that "remember?" is a pretty unnecessary tag on the end of the sentence, since one way or another, Nola needs to check her facts, and today she's checking her facts with me. I need to let Nola get her facts and leave it at that, all the while trying not to lose my temper with her.

One of the most disturbing aspects of James's traumatic brain injury is its impact on his short-term memory. Though he may enjoy a meal some relative or friend brought him from the tasty world outside of the nursing home and the beige cuisine therein, he will often complain moments after he finishes that he's hungry and ask why that same person did not bring him a sandwich. While he can clearly remember events from long ago, like my children's baptisms or joke about my clingy red dress that turned his face the same color, he cannot tell me for certain whether he had other visitors before I arrived on any given day. In an attempt to remedy this particular problem, James's mother placed a notebook and a pen in his room so that anyone who visited could sign in. Although it's often the same names appearing line after line, page after page, this log contains information that is much more reliable than James's memory. I find that I do not always challenge his recall by telling him that the notebook says his mother was indeed there just a few hours before I came. I'll just take a quick look and decide on the spot whether it would comfort James to know that she came or if it would just make him feel worse to know he doesn't remember her visit.

This whole forgetfulness thing is no doubt much more frustrating to the one who forgets than it is to me, irritated as I am with having to answer the same question way too many times or uncomfortable as I am to have to tell someone that they are wrong. I need to remember that this repetition is not malicious, that this person is probably not trying to make me want to scream, and that it must be pretty scary to not be able to trust your own thoughts.

Can we compromise? What if I just find another way to help Nola remember, if she can? Perhaps I could provide her a point of reference, like, "When we talked yesterday..." or "This morning when we were having breakfast..." or some other phrase that lets me help someone put the information in context while letting me let off just a tiny bit of steam before the next call about the same question? Or, if I don't wanna think too deeply about it, I could stop for a moment, try to detach a bit from my impatience and just answer the question for the fifth or sixth time.

What's "Normal" Anyway?

"I laugh, I love, I hope, I try, I hurt, I need,
I fear, I cry.
And I know you do the same things too. So
we're really not that different, me and you."
– Collin Raye

Sometimes I have to make a case to a class of undergraduate students who are resisting the idea that even if they don't become special education teachers, they need to know a few things about supporting children with disabilities. After all, children with disabilities are taught in all types of settings. I tell my students that they could be one life-changing event away from disability themselves. Do you think that statement's kinda harsh? "Yes, *you*, healthy young student, could sustain a brain injury from a car accident. *You* could give birth to a child who is later diagnosed with autism or maybe cerebral palsy at birth. *You* could have an accident out on the playing field and lose the ability to walk." The reality is that just about everyone will experience disability sometime during his or her life. As we age, the likelihood of having a disability of some kind increases, dear undergrads! Yes, guys, this means you! Get on board now!

Fortunately, I don't have to remind my students of this fact as much as I did when I first started teaching college. Hopefully, it's because I now use more subtle, effective means of getting my message across to my students than harsh words. Hopefully, it's because the ideas and initiatives that discourage separation of children with disabilities from their typical peers are working. Encouragingly, my students themselves have often been educated alongside peers with disabilities so they now often just assume all kids belong together because in their experience, they always did. As parent and author Kathy Snow says, "Disability is natural." Really, disability is just another way to *be*. Discomfort with difference seems to fade with steady contact. If a person with a disability is sitting next to me in math class, I will probably notice at first. Still, sitting next to me three months later, no biggie, it's normal. Steady contact makes disability mundane, just another type of normal.

And what does it mean to be *normal*, anyway? In my classes, as well as when I'm being mom, I try to refer to normal kids as *typical kids* or *typical peers*, but it's not as popular a term as the former. Is it worth differentiating between the two? In an attempt to figure out if there was a better word to ascribe to comparing children, I pulled up dictionary definitions for both *normal* and *typical*. I found that the two words had much in common, and sometimes even appeared as synonyms. Perhaps it's just a question of trying to choose a word that's a little less loaded, a little less common, a little less – you guessed it – *typical*, to shine light on the fact that there is no such thing as normal in humans, and perhaps we shouldn't act as if there is. You're normal for you, I'm normal for me, so no one is really normal. Yikes!

The writer Neil Marcus wrote of himself that his "Disability is not 'a brave struggle' or 'courage in the face of adversity'." He wrote that "Disability is an art, an ingenious way to live." Marcus is not romanticizing or glorifying disability; he's speaking from his own experience as a person with a disability. I hope that Nic's moments of generosity and courage, James's moments of patience and bravery, and my mother's times of struggle and perseverance are not held up as something beyond that of what any other typical person might have to go through – we all have these moments, though perhaps to a lesser extent. I hope that their lives are not something that separates them from others and makes them objects of pity or charity. Perhaps living with a disability really *is* a bit of an art, when one's working it, certainly often the crafting of an ingenious response to the challenges before the person. Nic uses the charm and the big brown eyes and the killer smile like weapons, and James finds ways around that weakened left hand when there is a cookie in that package and the wrapper's on tight. Nola makes a self-deprecating joke or simply disarms you with her charm when she can't quite recall what you ask her. I hope that somehow their struggles – and mine and yours – don't make a big point of our difference from others, but rather are attributes to our skill, our resourcefulness and the very essence of what makes us who we are. And I hope they remind us that we've all got struggles in our lives.

The other way I think about the term normal is the idea of living a *normal* life. For example, Nic gets angry, starts screaming, and knocks over a kitchen chair. The first time this outburst happened, Al and I were shocked and alarmed. Three or four knocked-over chairs later, however, this act became a common occurrence that we learned to physically and emotionally step away from; not *normal* behavior, but we've become accustomed to it. Knocking over chairs has now become a part of Nic's response repertoire and an unfortunate part of our home life. This behavior is a disturbing new *normal* for us, but we don't notice it after a while, because this expression of Nic's anger has come on so slowly, spread over a few months. In fact, we're only shocked and alarmed by the behavior when Nic does it outside of our home, like he'll be screaming and pitching kitchen chairs at Aunt Gail's house. We only realize Nic's behavior is "abnormal" again when we see that other people's kids don't scream and pitch large objects when they get mad; and we are then shocked as well as embarrassed by this behavior to which we had become desensitized over time. Even as I write, I feel terrible that I can use my own life for material on this particular topic, so beware the new *normal*.

But wait, there's still more to say about *normal*. Did you ever notice that people look less normal, less typical – whichever – when they are grouped by disability? Don't elderly people look older when you walk through a nursing home than when you see two of them sitting at a table in the Olive Garden having the unlimited soup-and-salad lunch among the other patrons of various ages? Don't people with significant cognitive or physical disabilities look more disabled when you see half a dozen of them and their staff in the mall food court than one person ina wheelchair does Christmas shopping with her friend and her sister at Target?

We have to keep an eye on *normal.* It can define anyone, but no two people wear it the same way. Normal is everywhere, but no one state of being defines it. Ha, *that's* normal.

So What Can You Do for Me?

"It is one of the beautiful compensations of
this life that no one can sincerely try to help
another without helping himself. "
– Charles Dudley

I may have learned this lesson about the challenges of others before there was a Nic or a James. I think I started learning it in 1987 after packing my bags and leaving my native New York City to try something completely different.

When I first arrived in Philadelphia, I lived pretty simply. In my first year there, I signed on to do full-time volunteer work at a shelter for homeless women in the heart of the Historic District. I lived in a row-house in the western, less glamorous part of Philly with three other volunteers on $150 a month each, plus room and board and a trolley pass. It was an interesting experience, but it was temporary. After finishing that one-year commitment, I was awarded a graduate assistantship at Temple University, to work on my master's degree and eventually my doctorate. My apartment cost me $175 a month, and I earned a salary based on working 20 hours a week at Temple (plus they paid my tuition; nice, but doesn't fill the belly).

To make ends meet, and because by now I was quite in the hole financially, I took another part-time job for the winter months, in an overnight shelter for homeless men, run by Sister Mary Scullion's Project H.O.M.E. Al, my fiancé at the time, led me to this job, since he was working for Project H.O.M.E., providing services to many of these same men – hardcore "street people" who stayed out all day and only came to the shelter for dinner, sleep and breakfast. Al and I ran this overnight shelter on Friday and Saturday nights in the basement of a community center in South Philadelphia. The shelter's only rules were: if you were caught with liquor, back out into the night you went; try to keep the noise down; and lights out was 11:00 PM.

That winter, I met a lot of people I would probably never have even noticed, men from everywhere, men who had done everything, veterans, former professionals and family men whose addictions had driven them away from their loved ones;; young men trying to get by and old men trying to get some rest. One of the younger men, a Vietnam veteran, was a graduate of the Ivy-est of the Ivy Leagues, but you wouldn't have guessed it seeing him on the corner by the church on 13thStreet, vacantly repeating, "Change? Change?" to passersby. In years to come, Al would recall various names to me, and tell me who had died over this winter or that, and I could still recall many of their faces. They had all been so kind to me, the soft-spoken graduate student who helped Al run the homeless shelter on Fridays and Saturdays.

I remember looking around the shelter one night and realizing that Al and I were completely outnumbered by these men in various states of exhaustion, inebriation, anger or despair. Our job was to get these 50 or so men fed, freshened up, bedded down, awakened, fed again and sent off to face another cold winter day on the streets of downtown Philadelphia. Taking my cue from Al, I said no to requests that violated the rules and yes to all offers of help from the men who volunteered them. After all, if many hands make light work, as Nola says, all clean hands would be welcome because there was breakfast to make for 50 at 6:00 AM and a disheveled community center to straighten up before we could all get out of there to start a new day.

I greatly appreciated the favors of the men who volunteered to help, but realized something else was happening when Bob, the former Navy cook from the Korean War, made the eggs for breakfast, or when Mike, who changed his name and affected a British accent when he hit the street, swept up after dinner. These men and several of the others who offered a hand seemed to be seeking a way to simply give back. They were doing something for Al and me and for their fellow guests, helping us to help them. In those simple acts of assistance, the men were productive, useful, helpful, skillful and very much appreciated, traits they probably did not demonstrate for much of the rest of their day. They really weren't expected to anymore.

I remember taking a few minutes to read the shelter log one evening when the men were asleep. I was surprised by the entries describing the many fistfights that broke out among these same gentle men, who were of so much help to Al and me. Some of the entries were made by employees Al and I knew personally, well-meaning workers who felt that these men should be helped by staff but not have to be of help to the staff because of their unfortunate situation. When I read those entries I always felt like the accomplice to my villain of a fiancé, but no-nonsense Al and I didn't have fights break out on our shifts, and the center was clean at 6:00 AM. Al and I were outnumbered and we knew it. We needed those men to help us, unfortunate situation or not – and they did.

I see this helping problem again and again in Nic and Nola, or perhaps more accurately, I see this problem in myself because of them. I am way too quick to do for my son and my mother what they can do for themselves, given the time and the presumption of competence that I am sometimes too rushed, stressed out, or simply too lazy to provide.

A psychologist once told me that Al and I learned to do everything for Nic years before, when he was that gravely ill infant who almost asphyxiated so many times. The doctor said it would take time for us to unlearn our overprotective response to him, and that it would take him time to stop expecting so much help from us as well. I find that this is still true to this day. Yet I can now take pride in Nic's assistance, in his willingness to help me empty the dishwasher, or feed the pets, or bring me a cup of water when I'm feeling sick. I know he takes pride in helping too. And when Nic needs the most reliable and indulgent place to be while mom and dad go do something else, I so often ask my Nola first. When she says yes, all is right in my world because the woman I trust most with my children is going to help me out today. She is doing something major for me, she who often needs so much help herself. Why shouldn't she?

What can someone who needs me do for me? Can I allow myself to accept what they give or do I assume that I shouldn't ask anything of them? Can I give them the time and the space to give it to me? Can I allow myself to enjoy and appreciate being on the receiving end? Yeah. Yeah, I really can.

Part 5 – Presence

Slow Down

"Teach us, O Lord, the disciplines of patience,
for to wait is often harder than to work."
– Peter Marshall

Nic coughed all night, the deep, persistent cough that keeps a parent on alert until morning. Now that I'm waking him to get him dressed for school, I find that he is hot all over. Today, the last day to hand in my grades for the semester. Today, when there's an all-school faculty meeting I'm supposed to attend to represent my department. Today, when Al can't stay home from work because he has to be in court. Today, I'm praying that Nic has an immediate spontaneous recovery despite what I see before me, and I'm not kidding. I am watching the clock and asking God to send down an angel to get him out of bed and turn down the body heat. I am wiping him down gently but hurriedly with a cool towel. Scarlet-cheeked and droopy-eyed, Nic is wilting on my shoulder. I am growing more and more anxious by the minute.

My prayer is answered. God sends an angel to get Nic out of bed but the angel just moves him onto my bed, where he falls right back to sleep.

I think that's the way it should have been, anyway. What was I thinking? It was like I had gone through those Elisabeth Kübler-Ross stages of grief – *denial/anger/bargaining/depression/acceptance* – over the loss of a day at work! It was clearly time to slow down and be present to this one person, my sick child, and that was the only activity there was going to be time for that day. So I take a deep breath, let go of my expectations, and Nic and I stay home.

As it turns out, Al comes home early, so although the faculty meeting never happens for me, I slip out and do my grades, just later in the day. Things work out.

. . .

Being with Nic always forces our family to slow down, sometimes willingly, sometimes with reluctance and frustration. He does just about everything more slowly; moving, speaking and talking in general. Knowing and accepting that this is the way it is can sometimes make it easier than trying to work against this basic truth about Nic. I'd like to say that slowing down for Nic makes me a better person, that I always see the benefit of moving more deliberately in the moment, and that I take time to stop and smell the roses, but my nose would grow like Pinocchio's. I get impatient, I get frustrated, I get sad, I get mad. But you know Nic and I always get there.

Driving to work that day with my newfound 20/20 hindsight, I felt foolish for thinking that Nic's fever would go away because I had other commitments. I felt guilty for this moment of bad priority setting, but I felt grateful for the opportunity it forced on me to take a reality check that day. What did I really have to do that was more important than taking care of my sick child? How did I get so caught up in my other obligations that I lost sight of what was happening right in front of me?

Slowing down, if I allow myself to do it, is about getting a chance to stop and think; and sometimes, if I really try, I actually do stop and I actually do think. It's the reason for long walks without being connected to a portable music player, for car rides with the radio off, and for getting to church a little early sometimes. In this instance, the reality of the sick child in front of me backed me into a corner, but I'm glad it did – even though I wasn't glad in the moment.

I once read a book called *CrazyBusy* just because I identified with the title. Well, actually, I listened to it on a CD in my car as one who tries to multitask might. I figured I could "read" the book and drive at the same time because I thought I was too busy to make time to finish a paperback version. It's a bit of the type of behavior the author calls "culturally induced ADD." This type of behavior, this level of divided attention, may very well keep a person from doing what matters most – in my case, taking care of a very feverish child. The author says that divided attention may even lead someone to do things they would otherwise deem unwise: in my case, it would be like sending Nic to school with a dose of Tylenol and keeping my fingers crossed that the nurse didn't call to send him home an hour after he arrived. Was that author guy looking in my window?

In some ways, Nic is perhaps my antidote to my sped-up lifestyle. If I can consciously adjust my speed to his sometimes, to that slower pace, I can get a little practice at being more present during moments that always last a little longer anyway with Nic.

Leave the Junk at the Door

"I myself am made entirely of flaws,
stitched together with good intentions."
— **Augusten Burroughs**

I know that spending time with James can be risky business; I have been welcomed warmly, offended deeply, sworn at occasionally, joked with over a shared snack, and growled at if I happen to arrive at the wrong moment. I have been asked to stay longer and told to get the hell out. I have been thanked for what I do and chastised for not doing enough. I have been told that my perfume is too strong and that the gel I use in my hair stinks, to the extent that I wear no perfume when I visit, and I take care to keep my curls out of sniffing distance. It's hard to know what to expect from this man on any given day. I don't get to flutter in on my angel-of-mercy-wings, and I'm not really comfortable with thinking of my time with him that way anyway. I don't feel that my time with James is about pity. I never think of my behavior as angelic. Sometimes, especially when I show up after a not-so-great day at work, home, wherever, whatever... I am just not that nice.

The junk? I bring home way home more work in my bag than I can complete at night. My purse is usually a landfill of receipts, tissues and leaky pens, to be sure. But that's not the junk I mean. It's my *emotional* junk – my worries, my anger, my sadness, my fear, my pain – that is not going to go away as I walk through the door without some deliberate intention on my part. I know I pick up on the moods of others like a sponge on a milk spill, so I figure that people may pick up on my moods too. I don't think it's too strange to be full of good intentions, at the same time being full of emotional junk, but I have to somehow shelve my junk here, at least temporarily. Letting it radiate out through my words and my demeanor is not going to make for an even mildly positive encounter.

Through a good bit of trial and error, I've found the best way to approach this need for self-control is to simply ask my junk to go away for a while, so I can be in this moment with this person. It's kind of like taking the Hippocratic friendship oath, on the way up in the elevator, to "first do no harm." Despite how odd it may look to the security guard watching the monitor from his office, hands in prayer, I ask God to bless the encounter on my way up to the fourth floor. I do it every time. I ask God to help me be a blessing, or at least not to make things worse by my presence. I ask God to help me be whatever God needs me to be, to do whatever God wants me to do, and to forget myself and my fragile ego a little, at least for now. If I am with someone to be a supportive presence, to be of some small comfort, as daughter, mother, or in this case, friend, I've given myself a little job beyond just showing up. I want to show up in a way that might even heal a little or comfort in some small way. I don't have to be a saint, just a slightly better mortal for an hour or two.

I'm not a superstitious person. I don't see asking for a blessing of the encounter as some kind of lucky charm, or that not asking for the blessing will make the visit go badly, like a chain email you're warned not to break, or else. I have had less than stellar visits with this same prayer, but as I look back on those visits, I wonder if I just didn't take my own words seriously enough to remember them and to choose to act on them through the rougher moments. Again, it's a prayer, not a talisman – it's a decision to be mindful of my effect on someone else.

One evening, a visit with James was pretty much circling the drain. There was lots of nasty banter, as though we were each trying to get the last, best, harsh word (in a soft voice, of course, because it's 9:00 p.m. in a nursing home). The conversation sometimes goes that way when James is in a bad mood, and the brain injury has a chance to take over and disinhibit his thoughts, so that even he can't seem to reign them in. In hindsight, after one too many meetings at work, I'd walked in pretty testy myself. I could feel my demeanor deteriorate, becoming more impatient and irritated as time passed. I knew I had just about enough and could easily make a sweeping drama queen exit in a sweeping drama queen huff.

Right there in the dimness of the room, I stopped and stepped away from the bed.

"Hi, Lord. This is not going so great. I'm sorry. Could you help us do a little better here?" I whispered. "Could you help this time end on a better note than it started?"

James must have wondered why I shut up so abruptly at that point. He was probably enjoying the silence.

Was it my awareness of the nature and demeanor of my presence in that moment that changed the course of the visit? Was it the prayer I slipped into the last moments of the visit that made a difference? Was it just a silence that allowed two people to break the mood? I don't know, but we parted better than we started. I think minimally, metaphorically, that I managed to push my junk back onto the elevator until it was time to go.

Ah, but what about the satisfaction of the alternative? The dramatic exit. Ooh, how delicious it would have been to get in that last biting word, to turn on my heel and storm out of there, to leave James gazing mournfully at the door, filled with sorrow and regret that his dear friend Gerry was gone.

Well, of course, first, there's always the chance that it wouldn't even register — James's memory fails him all the time, so I can't draw on any particular effect in him from which to draw some smug satisfaction. But there's always the chance that it *would* matter. What if some last offhand verbal swipe just made him feel as bad as me or maybe even worse? James has more than enough to feel bad about without me making it worse. What if I left another person feeling more hurt, or angry, or alone than if I'd never shown up at all? How awful would that be? Even if there's a slim chance that my words at that angry point would make a difference to James, it's me I have to live with. I need to do what I feel is the right thing to do, which is not always the satisfying thing for my ego in the moment.

Perhaps the real growth for me will be to ask James, or Nola, or Nic, to bless the encounter along with me, before the bad stuff happens or even while it's happening. I'll let you know how that goes. I'm new at this.

. . .

Leaving my junk at the door doesn't mean denying that I have problems – I certainly think I do have my share of problems, like everyone else. It means entering my house after a bad day at work and trying to greet my family lovingly, even though I will probably vent a little to Al about something or other in an hour or two when the kids aren't around. It means going into Nola's darkened bedroom on one of her very bad days and trying not to be anxious about all the tasks I was supposed to be attacking back home so I can be here in mind and spirit as well as in body to encourage my mother to get out of bed. In a perfect world, I will have made the situation a little better by my presence. The focus could be a gift to both of us – and after all, knowing that my presence made a situation worse would be nothing more than just junk for me to try to live with.

Eat Your Wheaties, There's Work to Do

"Life only demands from you the
strength you possess."
– Dag Hammarskjold

I've read somewhere that mothers of chronically ill children have shortened telomeres, the caps on the end of chromosomes, which indicate that the chronic stress of raising a child with exceptionalities of some kind could influence you at a cellular level. So if I think of Nic's constipation, seizure disorder, behavior disorders, asthma, diminished hearing, the anomalate artery closing his airway at 18 months, and all the other illnesses he's had that have put him in the hospital, the emergency room, or at least the doctor's office way more than his sister, I might have shortened telomeres more so than the average mom (never mind what it's done to Nic). So not just my looks, my patience, my scrambled memory, but my very *cells* can be affected – yikes! No fair! And by definition it looks like I also qualify as a member of the "sandwich generation," taking care of my children and helping to provide support to my elderly parents, plus, I work full-time… I don't know when last I've been able to say I had nothing to do.

Fortunately, the research has not decreed that the lives of people like me have to be unhappy, constantly super-stressful, or God forbid, shorter. The trick is that I'm supposed to take care of myself while I take care of the usual mom-wife-working-woman-stuff, plus the extra challenges of being a parent of a complicated child and a daughter of a mother who is struggling. Research says I don't have to look as bad as I sometimes feel, and I can allow someone else to take care of it (whatever *it* is) sometimes. Research says I don't need a week's vacation to feel better, either; sometimes I just need a half hour by myself upstairs with a good book. I agree, but if it was that easy I'd have done it already. Sometimes even thinking about how to lessen your stress can be stressful. Where do I start?

As a caregiver who is trying to keep balance in her life, I also need to find people with whom I can share my story, a person or two who doesn't need all the details recapped every time we talk; just some people who "get it." My friend Kate refers to these people as my "select few." I'm a lucky old girl on this one. I have some friends who are also in the sandwich. I have some friends who have kids with disabilities. And I have a lot of friends who are just so very wise. I also have my family – my sister, my brother, my cousin Renee (and our two-hour phone conversations), and dear, dear, long-suffering Al. My select few are the ones whom I can call with the ugly stuff and trust that my angry, my hurt, my "crazy" stays with them. I need these people. We all need these people. Just getting things out of my head and into the air, in the form of spoken words, is a tremendous stress reliever for me. Often, my stories sound worse in my head than when I say them out loud. And nothing I've confided to those who "get it" has shocked any one of them off their chair or ruined a perfectly nice lunch date. I do my best to hold up my end of the deal, to be the ear for someone else's anger, and their hurt, and their crazy too. It's a work in progress.

. . .

It seems that you don't burn out from spending a lot of time with people who are suffering – you burn out from your efforts to ignore or hold in the stress from the suffering that you've already absorbed. If suffering is a kind of ongoing bad news, I know I have a real aversion to bad news. I don't even like to read the evaluations my students do of my courses at the end of a semester just in case someone didn't think I did a good job teaching. And forget about getting on a scale. I don't know when the last time *that* was good news.

When I think about the type of information I ignore or repress about Nic or Nola, like their bad news, it often has to do with what I see them going through. It has to do with how helpless I sometimes feel about how to support them and how bad I feel that they sometimes need support more than I can give. But what can I do about someone else's struggles if I can't admit that in some way they cause me suffering too? I have one other thing to deal with here, I need to see the truth of the situation from both sides, not just my own.

Maybe it would be better not to continue to cling to a definition of my relationship with Nola as "mother and child," even though the changes are relatively recent. I know that she realizes she might be throwing her children's lives off course right now. She says this to me from time to time and I don't have any kind of wise response to offer beyond, "Don't worry about it." She is, at some level, correct, whether it matters or not. My mother also knows, at a level she would probably never admit to herself or me, that she is somewhere at the mercy of Mike, and Gail, and me – I mean, after all, who hires the help? Who decided help had to be hired? Who gave who power of attorney?

The sibs and I are in this for the long term. Our parents have the gift of long lives that were denied to the parents of many of our friends and family. At times it is frustrating to hear Nola complain about this gift, as her particular length of days seem to be distressing to her now. It is as conflicting to take some of her phone calls as it is to let some go by because I'm just not up to them right now. But here we are, and this is no time to add to Nola's sorrows by letting her know that sometimes her anxiety/depression/dementia trifecta completely freaks me out. I am working on that, one encounter at a time.

Maybe my telomeres won't shorten as much if I make sure that I'm taking care of myself physically, emotionally and spiritually. We're all supposed to anyway, right? There are TV and magazine empires built on that concept! It seems like much more of a conscious effort than it was even a few years ago. Life is busy. Maybe if I do a little better for myself then I can help someone else take care of themselves, too. For me, I find that rather than attacking every level of self-care at once, it sometimes helps to just pick one at a time. I know that when I exercise, I just plain feel better – I hear that has to do with creating more endorphins in my brain or something. (I wonder if it does anything for shortened telomeres?) I don't even have to work out for long periods of time that I don't have anyway. I just have to do it consistently (uh-oh). Like how if I ask my husband to turn off the TV in our bedroom a little sooner, I can make time to pray or be silent just before I go to bed. I'm giving myself a little spiritual care here, though this request usually makes Al squirmy enough to bolt for the living room TV. After a while, I start to feel like I am the Dalai Lama, all deep in prayer in my candlelit room, but I also do sleep better. Taking care of myself is not supposed to be a guilty pleasure; I can't act like I'm treating myself to a walk or a good night's sleep. Taking care of myself is an obligation to me and the people I encounter, especially if they are struggling and might need me to step up for them at some point. I have to take care of myself so that I can be a healthier version of me and not make others' situations worse by my stressed-out, agitated, short-tempered presence, at least a little less often.

This, though, is my favorite and easiest way to remember it: A person's needs are met best by people whose needs are being met.

Listen for Truth

"Be a person who listens and does not take away my struggle by trying to make it all better."
— **Norman Kunc**

Years ago, when I would visit my beloved 94-year-old godmother in the nursing home in New Jersey where she lived after leaving the Bronx, she'd sometimes say reflectively, "This is the end of the line for me, you know. I won't be leaving here." In my zeal to comfort her and to keep things perky and upbeat, I'd always be quick to dismiss that statement, saying that no, it probably wasn't the last place she'd live; that who knew what the future could bring. I didn't want her to be sad or give up hope, or feel resigned to her rather marginal existence, so I opted for big-time Pollyanna optimism.

I mentioned these conversations between my godmother and me to a woman I worked with at lunch one day. After listening to what I thought were the comforting words I'd offered my godmother, my coworker thought a moment and responded, "But it probably *is* the end of the line for her. Why would you tell her that it's not?"

Good question. My godmother was very old, not so well anymore, and she had outlived her husband and both of her sons. Why did I need to dismiss her statement as too gloom-and-doom only to replace it with something pleasant but highly unlikely? The nursing home probably was the last place she'd live, meaning, of course, that our time together was soon to end. Maybe I just didn't want that to be true, but my godmother deserved to have her say. She deserved to speak her truth.

Listening to Nola, when she's feeling low, can be just plain frustrating. So many things I can't fix. There's nothing new to tell here;

Nola's angry with herself for not being able to remember information the way she once could. I can't fix that. Nola doesn't want to go anywhere or do anything, she just stays in bed. I can't fix that. Nola is "annoyed", her new favorite word, with everything, more than a few people, and with herself. She repeatedly tells me, "I just want to get back to being myself." At this point, suggesting to her that she and my dad should come over or that I'll stop by, is often met with a dismissive "No", as though I'd said something absolutely ridiculous. And heaven help us if there's a social obligation, like a dinner, when she's feeling like this. The very environment that brings my mother out of her shell, the very charm she releases effortlessly in a group, is the thing that she cannot bring herself to evoke when she's feeling low. But since it is hard for me to hear that, I sometimes decide not to listen. I just want to yell, "Oh, snap out of it! You're fine, just get your skinny butt over here!" I don't want to believe that she's struggling; moms are supposed to always be strong for their children, even their middle-aged children. But she deserves to have her say, Nola deserves to speak her truth.

I heard what my godmother said, and I hear what Nola says, but I didn't like the messages, so I didn't do a very good job of listening to them.

I think that listening well is about realizing how really, really hard it is to give someone your full attention, especially when you don't like their message – but making the effort anyway. I've talked to my sophomores and juniors about the gift of the good listener or the ability to be one as a trait to nurture in teachers, but I'm not sure where I fit in on that spectrum myself, sometimes. People like me don't always listen well, perhaps because it is too much work, or perhaps because there is so much I'm thinking about saying as I'm trying to listen that I just can't keep my attention on what they're saying. That is embarrassing to admit.

The difference between hearing and listening is the difference between reality and *my* reality. When they're not the same thing, I push for my version because I need my version. I prefer a happy mother. In these moments of a struggling mom or a godmother at the end of her journey, the truth is scaring me. Changes are coming that I'm not going to like, so I'm just not gonna pay attention. Huh. Take that, truth!

Maybe it isn't going to be all right by my standards. Maybe what I want is *good*, but not ultimately the *best*. Maybe it doesn't matter what I want just now. I have to grow into this new situation with my mother. I have to listen to Nola's truth, even the parts that don't seem true, or the parts that I don't want to be true.

Am I changing in all of this? I realize, I simply have to pay attention, so that's a start. Who am I becoming? Who have I *become* since I started considering the parallels and the changes in the ways that I'm present to Nola, Nic and James? Can all this caregiving make me a better teacher? A better wife? A better friend? Or is it a linear path that cuts through the rest of my life and heals without leaving a mark that tells the world that I grew up a little in these last three years?

Normally, I try hard to give my attention and presence to friends who are struggling. I want to make their problems go away, and I want to say the magic words that will do it. There's something that's supposed to be comforting about telling someone in trouble that "It'll be all right." I do it all the time, but who am I saying that for? I'm supposed to be comforting someone else with these words, but I'm not so sure about them these days. I know when I've poured my heart out about whatever immediate crisis I happen to be in and someone says, "Ah, don't worry. It'll be all right," no matter what their tone or their intention, I generally want to throw my purse at them. I feel dismissed, a little patronized, and not a bit better. Telling someone "It'll be all right" doesn't speak to the present, and what they want to talk about, which is how they are feeling, which is probably crappy. This type of response is not doing the work of loving presence that I need to be doing, nor is it giving the attention that could actually be meaningful and helpful to the person to whom I'm speaking. I may get better at listening in time, but it will always require an effort for me.

So I'm trying to amend the "It'll be all right," by listening a little harder to what the *it* is. I generally really want to say these words because I really believe that ultimately things will be all right; we just don't know what "all right" looks like as yet. My friend Lynetta's mother says that "You can see to the corner, but God can see around the corner." Much as I like and believe what she's saying, that particular turn of the phrase doesn't quite sound like it would come out of me. I'm gonna go for a phrase that looks a little more like this: "I think it will be all right (if I really do). It just isn't right now. But I'm here for you." Depending on the audience, I may use the slightly coarser, "It just sucks right now" before adding "but I'm here for you." Then I'll try to shut up and let them talk some more – and listen to what they are saying.

Perhaps the other important idea to remember, if I'm going to try to say something comforting, is that I probably know more about the person to whom I'm speaking than I do about the situation. I might know what they're good at, what they care most about, what I admire most in them. Can I use that? What can I say to let them know that I believe in them and that I'm rooting for them? On several occasions, I have simply told James that he is hands down the toughest person I have ever met. I sincerely mean that, so it leaps to mind immediately. The man died three times in the emergency room, which I often fall back on as supporting data. That's fairly tough in my opinion, so, I throw it in as needed. When Nola tells me that her moments of cheery demeanor are all an act because she feels so bad, I tell her that I think in those moments she truly *is* "her old self", the self she's always looking to become again; and that I love seeing the "old" Nola, act or not. By the way, I believe that it may start as an act for Nola, but her gradual cheering up in a crowd is like warming up a car before you take it out on the road; once it's running, it's running!

I'm giving it a try, this little bit of guarded optimism. Closer to the truth, maybe. More in the right-this-minute, definitely. It's my best effort at listening a little better even when I don't like what I'm hearing. I need to let people speak their truth.

They Have Junk, Too

*"If you kick us down in anger, you
will hurt your own foot."*
– Korean Proverb

I almost did it, but I stopped myself because I knew I would regret it.
Tonight, I got called some names that no one has ever called me,
horrible, hurtful names, and I'm not even sure why. The words kept
coming, like he did not want to, or perhaps could not, stop.

I almost did it, but I stopped myself. It was like this with James
once before, this unbridled hostility that became a sure sign that it was
time for me to step back 'cause there was nothing else to do. But this
time even I was shocked by the coarse words I heard coming out of
him, and I thought I was pretty shock-proof by this point.

I almost did it, came so close to doing it, but I stopped myself. In
my restraint, I started feeling that on this night I was a woman in the
wrong place at the wrong time. I could've been anyone and gotten a
mouthful this night, but it was me, it was here and now, and I got it
baaaad.

I almost did it but I stopped myself because it was wrong and I'd
regret it. It was right there by the bed, and I reached for it, and touched
it, but I pulled back. That ever-present Styrofoam cup of ice water –
James asked for a drink, and I so wanted to just pitch it at him. Funny
how someone could call you all those terrible names and then not think
twice about asking for your help. A symptom of the larger problem of
the brain injury, the resulting disinhibition of thought, the crushing
despair of the situation, I'm guessing. But at that moment, I was rapidly
losing my well-practiced caring demeanor. I left my junk at the door

like I always tried to, but, oof, I was shocked, I was hurt, I was mad as hell that James would verbally ambush me. He had an ice bath coming, but I pulled back from grabbing that Styrofoam cup.

A couple of months before, James received a bit of a reprieve from the nursing home, spending two weeks in an intensive stroke rehab program. Two weeks off the fourth floor of the nursing home, two weeks of new faces, two weeks of hard physical and mental work. He and his family and I had all hoped and held our breaths in anticipation of a positive outcome from the program, even a few small steps in a better direction (dare we say in the direction of home over nursing home). In the end, however, the medical consensus was that nothing cognitive or physical had really changed. Rehab did not turn out to be the end of an era for James; he wasn't gonna go home into his mother's house when it was all done, as he'd hoped. It was back to the nursing home, back to the fourth floor, same long empty days, the same pain, the same isolation, same everything, or perhaps more accurately, the same almost-nothing.

Sometimes I dunno how James gets up in the morning at all, but I suppose he doesn't really have a choice. He was frustrated, unhappy and so terribly disappointed at the decree that he had ostensibly flunked rehab. The program probably could not address both the effects of the brain injury and the impact of the number of strokes he had since, so the whole experience was over very quickly.

Ooh, but the level of name calling that night? It was the stuff of which ice-water immersions are made. He had it coming. But I stopped myself because I knew I'd regret it. Hand firmly placed in pocket, fist clenched.

So I collected myself and I left the darkness of the room. Walking quickly toward the fluorescent light of the hallway, I told myself aloud I wouldn't be going back to see James for a while. In my parting words, I told him in the calmest tone I could muster that I would never give up on him. I told him I'd keep him in my prayers, then I was gone. It was all I could do in the moment. There was like tension in what felt like every muscle in my body as I kinda held back tears I never would let him see on me. I didn't blame him for being frustrated, sad, depressed, all that, and I told him as much as I stood to leave. But it can't be all right to be spoken to like that. Having pain does not make it okay to inflict pain. It is hard not to take it personally (especially when the words were so exquisitely personalized), but I will try. I didn't cry or anything, but I haven't stopped thinking about it since.

I wonder if it would've been satisfying to pour that ice water on James's head – ha, duh, yes! – but probably only in the instant. Would that have been worth it? I'd have probably been ashamed of myself five seconds later. The deep-throated scream that would've come from his shock at both the act and the water temperature would definitely have gotten me kicked out of the nursing home, maybe for good. I did manage to perform one tiny act of the hissy fit drama before I exited, though. I had to do with something to express my anger and hurt, after all. So with great flourish and a few choice mutterings under my breath, I plucked off every photo on his wall with me or my children in it. I shoved them into the bottom drawer of his night table and slammed it shut so hard that the drawer bounced back open, ('cause I needed a little theater).

In the moment, I felt the urge to launch into some loud diatribe about how I'd been there for him all this time, and have taken him places, advocated to others for him, fed him all the junk he shouldn't have, cut his hair, decorated his room for the holidays, on and on and on. But I know I hadn't done all that stuff for him alone, really. I did what I did for him because it made me feel right about being there. I never asked to be thanked, so why bother to throw that out there in this angry moment? Obviously we were both in some pain, but mine was temporary; I was leaving for a happier place, but James wasn't going anywhere.

· · ·

I was the obvious target that night, but I'm not sure I was the real target. Maybe I wasn't even the only target that day, and maybe it wasn't about a human target at all. But what would it have gained for me or him to lash out and trash him back? As personal as it all was, somewhere I knew it just wasn't about me. It was about pain, as well as real, physical, mental, emotional, no-way-out despair and disappointment. It was "You can't help me, no one can help me, I'm trapped, my life is over, I wish I was dead" pain. But it doesn't make it okay for anyone to speak to anyone else with hatred and derision, and so it's break time, for my sake and perhaps for James's sake too.

Cherish Quiet Moments

"Leave a tender moment alone."
– Billy Joel

When my daughter Courtney was small, her bedtime ritual always included prayers by the bedside and a reading of a picture book all curled up with daddy or mommy. Al and I read to her way past the time when she could read for herself, because it was just such a lovely time to be with our child in the quiet coziness of her bedroom. Everything had been done for the day. There was nothing left but a good story and a goodnight. I still miss those days. Now it's most often a TV show until bedtime, immersion in a novel all her friends are reading, texting her friends from her cell phone, or all three at the same time. Sometimes it's even homework.

I still get to love the end of the day with Nic the way I once did with Courtney. One of the reasons I can indulge in story time, even now that he is so much older, is that Nic does not read very well on his own. As with my daughter, parent and child will usually enjoy a book together, though lately the bedtime story has given way to lists of trivia about favorite members of Nic's beloved Philadelphia Phillies in their annual yearbook. At least it's age appropriate and relatively educational in a pop-culture kind of way.

Mother and child say a prayer together next. Nic blesses our family, his teachers, his friends, his friends' mothers for some reason, and all of our pets. It's a great time to talk about the day as well as a really great time to not talk about the day. Nic doesn't always settle down right away, so sometimes I'll grab a pillow and stretch out on the floor beside his bed. I really don't need to do this, and he's way too old for this type of coddling, but it's so dark and so quiet except for the sound of his breathing that sometimes it feels like a little bit of an indulgence for me to just be still and quiet for a few minutes. After all, I should probably be downstairs finishing up the dinner dishes, or putting in a load of wash now that it's after 9:00 p.m. and the energy rates are down, but I've chosen to lie down on the floor beside my child instead, hoping that Al will remember the laundry and maybe throw in some darks.

. . .

In the morning it will be completely stressful to rouse the kids out of their beds at 6:00 a.m. and hustle them to their respective school buses. Courtney will remain curled up under her comforter until the last possible moment, then somehow try to shower and style her hair in the 10 minutes she has left. In addition, I will have to physically snag her at the door to hand off a glass of milk, gummy vitamins and a bag of dry cereal so she'll eat some kind of breakfast as she dashes to the bus. Simultaneously, Nic will scream that he doesn't wanna go to school, sometimes hurling himself to the floor in an enraged heap rather than going to the bathroom to get washed up. He will aggressively resist brushing his teeth and combing his hair. We will get a good breakfast into him, however, because Nic just loves sausage and scrambled eggs with lots of ketchup. He may willingly walk to the bus or he may yell some more and take an angry swing at one of us if he is really mad. Thank God for patient bus drivers who just wait out the tantrum so that we can calm him down and get him out the door. At 7:00 a.m., when Courtney and Nic are both on their way to school, I would like to just run upstairs and swan dive back into my bed, but I have a 9:30 class to teach and a long commute north to the university.

Cherish quiet moments? They are the only things that get me through the many crazy moments. And there's not much lovelier than a warm blanket, a read-aloud book and a sleepy child.

Forgiveness is a Good Option

"It's our choices... that show us what we
truly are, far more than our abilities."
– J.K Rowling

On the last night of the summer session class I was teaching at the university, I stopped at the nursing home on my way home. Yeah, I did. It was a mere six days later, not the "I won't be going back for a *while*," that I had declared in anger and hurt over the harsh words that James had said to me on my last visit. Those harsh words had not left my mind, and the emotion they evoked had not dissipated during the break I had tried to impose on myself. I didn't like what I was thinking about over those six days, and that I was hanging on to those thoughts and endlessly batting them around in my mind. At this rate, the break would last forever and it wouldn't be in any way a break for me. I felt like a finalist, if not the outright winner, of the Miss Pathetic Masochist Pageant. Or maybe some kind of trauma groupie. Enough already.

The situation at this point reminded me of the story of a Buddhist monk who was robbed at gunpoint in a bus station. At first, the monk felt great rage but as time went on, he began to feel great compassion for the robber, to the point of tears. When he told one of his students the story, the student wondered why the monk would feel compassion after all he'd been through. The monk replied, "If I'd lived that man's life and had the experiences he's had, I would have been the one pointing the gun." Forgiveness is maybe less about reconciliation and more about simply letting go of anger in the moment when you try to look at an experience through someone else's eyes.

And so, hoping that I was more than a glutton for punishment, I tried to replace that endless angry thinking and the feelings that came with them with a little prayer – actually, lots and lots of prayer and positive energy – instead. I had to stop the thoughts when they came in and do something else besides ruminate in them. I had to substitute them with thoughts I could live with until I decided what to do next. I didn't know what to pray for so I just asked for blessings for James and openness to what the future held here for me, if indeed this were truly another ending point for our friendship. But instead of leading me away from the problem and relaxing me so that I could really take a break, my intentions seemed to move me back toward what had happened, where it happened, and of course, with whom.

Even in the car on the way home from work, I asked God whether I should stop in or not; hell, I already knew where I was heading next. What I didn't know was what would await me there. More of the same verbal thrashing? I needed to be ready, whatever that meant. More harsh words were a very real possibility, but then what? Still couldn't drown the man with a Styrofoam cup of ice water. Even weirder, would this encounter that had so upset me be lost on him? Would this memory of the occurrence that had possessed me fail him while I was endlessly reliving it? Would James remember, but not care? Nothing to hope for here, but into his room I walked quietly, my junk placed at the door as best I could secure it.

Through the crack in the bedroom door I could see James being assisted with preparing for bed. He called out to me from the all-important restroom where he must have caught a glimpse of me as well, passing by on my way to the far corner of his bedroom. I had never heard him call out to me before. The nurse helped him finish putting on his hospital gown, then held his side and walked with him into the room to support him into his bed. Watching him struggle to walk commanded my attention, as it always did. I nodded a greeting and sat myself down in a recliner a few feet away, not on the floor beside the lowered bed as I usually did.

What was I gonna do now? I had nothing to say, no monologue planned to review with him the events of the week before. I mean, whose bright idea was this? So I just sat and said nothing. 5 minutes passed, 10 minutes, 15 minutes, not a sound. Not a sound but the TV and two people breathing in a now darkened room. No motion but that of characters moving across the screen.

As I sat wordless and still, I began to ask for blessings and positive energy. I closed my eyes and stretched my arms out on the chair, palms toward James. I occasionally practice yoga and hands-on healing – more reasons I like to refer to all of this as positive energy as well as prayer. I was feeling all Dalai Lama-ish. I was no longer particularly aware of anything except a feeling of something radiating through me. Maybe it was a little peace returning after six days of agitation. I tried not to doze off, which happens sometimes when I get all Dalai Lama-ish, especially in a recliner.

Finally, a stirring: James requested water (brave guy!). I walked over and offered the cup, and he took a sip. I sat back down, TV droning, me asking for blessings and openness. Ten minutes later, another request. I offered the cup. He took a sip. I sat back down. Not a sound but prime-time programming and the hum of central air.

About a half hour had passed now, but I felt comfortable just being silent like we were. I felt okay about not trying to make conversation with James, though I would have loved to bring up the topic of the verbal thrashing of days before. There needed to be a different path here, and I was gonna take that path, even if it made me grind my teeth smooth to do it. Just being in the moment, letting it unfold, sitting in a comfy chair on the other side of the room – trying that different way, a way containing absolutely nothing but open space.

So after a few more minutes, it did indeed feel like it was time for me to leave. I was coming out of my deep place, and I actually felt just a little refreshed, as though my heart had fallen away. I did what I came to do, to just pray into the situation. Somehow my air felt a little clearer and my heart a little lighter even though nothing had changed. I stood up, stretched and swung my pocketbook over my shoulder. Taking a few steps toward the bed, I whispered goodnight and stepped back.

James turned his gaze away from the TV and looked up at me.

"I feel bad," he said. Well, he doesn't usually feel well, of course, but I was surprised by this personal remark after such a night of silence.

Perhaps his stomach? Maybe his head?

"What bad, like sick?" I asked.

"I feel bad," he repeated.

"Well, bad about what?"

"I'm not sure," he answered, lowering his eyes. "I think I feel bad about something I said to you."

"Really?"

He looked up at me now. "I should never have said what I did. I'm so sorry. I hope some day you'll forgive me."

Well, an apology wasn't supposed to happen here. He has short-term memory loss, righty? This was all supposed to be lost on him. I think I gasped a little.

I took another breath, taking in his words as well. I had no clever response to this one, surprised as I was. "Done," I said. I looked down at my feet and back at him, and felt a small little smile creep over my face.

"Alright, well, good night, Father." Feeling a need for a moment to distance myself from my own sudden change of heart, I just didn't feel like calling him *James*.

"What'd you say that for?"

"What? Good night, Father?"

"After all the time I've known you?" Caught. He heard it, too.

"What, still prefer James?"

"No. 'Slob'," he said with a little smile. "Or 'Immature'."

Well, I had to laugh a little. "I, I think I'll stick with James."

"I like you."

"I like you, too," I said.

"Next time, bring pizza."

. . .

So I'm learning that it's a lot better to try to forgive, or at least to let go of hurt, than it is to hold on to feelings that are painful and troubling. The writer Anne Lamott says, "Not forgiving is like drinking rat poison and waiting for the rat to die." A perfect, if somewhat graphic, analogy.

That sounds about right. For me, such hurt, troubled feelings always grow into full-blown obsessions, taking on a life larger than the situation from whence they came. I realize that I can't assume I really know what someone else is thinking or going through, or what made them do or say what they did. It's probably not worth over-analyzing because that's not where the truth is gonna be found anyway. I'm learning that there's something to my leave-my-junk-at-the-door mantra and entering into the situation with an open mind. And it is especially useful when there's a lot of junk in both minds. I'm learning that you just never truly know what another person's thinking, and that things aren't always what they seem. That phrase is easy to say, but sometimes a little hard to believe in the moment. To "presume competence" is to remember that there is truth in these moments, but it must be tempered with openness to what stands in the way of the delivery of that truth.

And I'm learning that in the difficult moments, we really don't go it alone. Before I left James that night, I noticed that the photos I'd angrily slammed into the bottom drawer of his night-table had all been put back up on the walls. I don't know who did it, but there they were, push-pinned in their usual spots near James's bed.

Can Anything I Might Say Beat Silence?

"It is a great thing to know the season
for speech and the season for silence."
– Seneca

In a small and shaky voice, Nola asked me if she had Alzheimer's. She and I were waiting for the visiting nurse who was coming to do an evaluation for in-home companion care. By definition, it seems she does not have that particular type of dementia, but why should she believe me right now? After all, we were waiting for a visiting nurse. I wrapped my arm around my mother's shoulder and whispered, "No."

Life at my parents' house has changed a lot lately. My mother recently suffering a huge bout of depression, took to her bed and stopped doing just about everything. She didn't cook for herself or my father. The clothes hamper overflowed with laundry. Nola stopped going for her evening walks and stopped visiting her friends. She stayed in her pajamas and her little pink foam hair rollers. My mother drew the blinds in her bedroom and pulled the drapes shut. She made calls to her children in a weak and desperate voice that totally freaked us out. "Oh, Gerry (or Gail, or Mike,)" she'd sigh. "What's wrong with me?"

My father went out to the garage and puttered, confused and troubled by yet another change in his wife.

Eventually, in the late summer, Mike and I called 911, fearing dehydration. It was the last desperate resort of children who truly did not know what was wrong with their mother. In minutes, the ambulance pulled up silently, as is the custom in our parents' 55 and over community. Nola slipped on a clean blouse, ran a comb through her silver hair and walked down the hall and out the door. She acknowledged the waiting stretcher only when it was inevitable. It reminded me of Blanche DuBois at the end of *A Streetcar Named Desire* when Stanley Kowalski betrayed her, with Mike and me sharing the role of Stanley.

I cried.

In the ambulance, however, Nola immediately began to chat casually with the EMT, as he and I perched on opposite sides of her gurney. She queried him cheerfully about his family as he took her blood pressure, talked about her past experiences taking Nic to the ER in this same ambulance 10 years before. She made jokes about what she was gonna do to me for making her go to the hospital in an ambulance in front of the whole neighborhood.

After the nurses examined Nola head to foot and asked a multitude of questions, it turned out that she had not been taking one of her antidepressant medications. No one knows how such a glaring error got by us. The medication was not the type you could stop cold turkey but Nola had done just that, whether she meant to or not. Within a few days, restoration of the correct dosage returned her to a better state, still not her "old self", but the blinds and the curtains in her room are open again. In the meantime, my sister, my brother and I have become the cooks, preparing and leaving 12 boxed meals in my parents' refrigerator each week, healthy snacks for grazing, double checking the meds with my father and popping in the occasional load of laundry.

What was I to tell her as she stood with me in the bathroom waiting for the doorbell to ring? Did she have Alzheimer's? Technically no, but she had something, or else there wouldn't be a nurse coming to check her vital signs and ask us a bunch of questions today. Would anything I could say in answer to such a question ever be an improvement over silence? And who's to say I'd be correct? I gave her the "no" she seemed to need, and that I needed to believe as well. We held each other and silently waited for the nurse.

. . .

James has skin cancer. He's had a few melanomas here and there for as long as I've known him. When a growth is malignant, he gets it removed. Years before, I remember buying him pure vitamin E oil because he was so concerned about the scar the surgery was going to leave on his jaw, detached that he was in that priestly way from worldly stuff like little scars on the side of your jaw.

That old scar is nothing compared to the two-inch gash this latest malignant melanoma removal left down the center of his cheek. No hiding this scar, but the scar seems hardly a big deal in light of what else has happened to him in these last couple of years. What I notice, more than the mark down his cheek, is the change in his demeanor after the operation to remove the malignancy. Did this procedure leave one wound too many? Was it a bad idea to be anesthetized after a brain injury and several strokes? There wasn't really any choice about the need to remove a malignancy: He had to go under the knife and he had to be knocked out to do it, but something is different.

I stopped by the nursing home on a Wednesday afternoon on the way home from work, a very large turkey hoagie in my hand, a can of diet Coke in the other. Settling in as always, I offered to share half my sandwich with James and he, of course, agreed. By the look on his face as he examined it though, the sandwich was way too whole-wheaty (the way I like it) and with the wrong type of cheese (the kind I like) and oil instead of mayo (the way I like it) but he grudgingly took a piece anyway. So, we sat quietly with our hoagie halves, balancing paper, sandwich and beverage on a rolling lunch tray in front of James, watching TV's Judge *somebody-or-other*, listen to people air their personal complaints for the world to hear.

When we finished eating our hoagie halves, I began to clean up our table. I tossed the hoagie paper into the trashcan and pushed the little rolling tray away from us. The wheel of the tray hit James on the backside of his foot, which was well-encased in big, black sneakers.

Before I could say, "Whoops," he punched me so hard on my upper arm that I flinched.

"Hey, what was that for?" I shouted.

"You hit my foot," he replied flatly.

I must say I was shocked. The man punched me! Pretty strong guy still! What on *earth*...?

Well, the conversation deteriorated from there, and it wasn't a long one. I still refrained from a visceral response, as with the other very unpleasant visit of a few months back. *That* would've given me a delicious but temporary satisfaction, this time with my purse so heavy and James's head so ripe for an accidental whack. He seemed at once to want to make a joke of hitting me but added that in no way did he believe the cart had run into his foot by an accident. I flung my handbag over my shoulder and left, more sure than ever that something else had been lost in James after that operation. I'm wondering if the next thing he needed to lose was the increasingly-more-difficult visits from me.

I didn't spend a lot of energy mulling over this episode after it was over. It just happened, this sad, ridiculous incident. It deepened my concern over what was becoming of James physically and mentally more than anything. I started to feel like the man I knew, the priest, the friend, the lunch buddy, was simply beginning to disappear right in front of me. If he was truly disappearing, I realized that it did not give me license to do the same. I knew better than to take this incident personally. All there was to do was to let go of the hurt feelings. The sore arm wouldn't last either. All that was left to do was hang in.

I said a prayer for him that evening, in the car on my way home.

. . .

Hey, if I'm committed to a cause or a person, they are never far from my mind even when I try to push them away. I sometimes wish I could just let them go, already. Then I could tell myself that what they did drove me away from them and that would be that. But even then, it's just a matter of my choosing in what way they would remain with me – as they are or as some kind of enemy – because I know they're in me either way. I have to find my peace, and for me, everyone in my life seems to eventually have a place in that peace. I'm always gonna take my mother's calls, even over my own protests – at least the first five of the day, anyway.

So, I went back to the nursing home the next night after work. James was in the dark, lying in bed. I said hi and sat down in the comfy chair by the radiator. He asked if I had a soda. Nope, no soda. He asked if I had a pizza. Yeah, forget that for a while.

"No, no pizza. I just brought myself."

I sat in that chair, opened my hands and repeated to myself, "Oh, peace and blessing to this room and everyone in it" over and over until a feeling of peace came to me, and hopefully to him as well. I stayed for 15 minutes, said goodbye, and back into the night I went.

I think my definition of presence changed that evening. It expanded into the singular, the intangible, the wordless. I wasn't looking for anything but peace. There was no sense of reciprocity, no expectation at all. It felt as though this visit was the way it needed to be just then, perhaps for a while to come, and maybe it was gonna stay that way. What could I have said that would've been an improvement over silence in this moment? In those 15 minutes, it felt like the presence it needed to be. James was quiet, I was quiet. A little less James, a little less me. Just a little prayer. Hopefully it was enough for that moment.

That night I had a dream about James. He told me it was time for him to go. He stood up from his wheelchair, kissed and hugged me, then he said goodbye.

I didn't expect that at all.

Sometimes I Feel Like a Giant Failure

"In the middle of the journey of our life I
came to myself within a dark wood where
the straight way was lost."
– Dante Alighieri

This is the part where I take a moment to sulk, to pout, and to throw myself a three-page pity party. This is the chapter where I admit that I don't want my mother to be elderly and depressed and anxious and need lots of help from Mike, and Gail, and me. This is the chapter where I let the answering machine take her fifth call while I go eat a large piece of red velvet cake. This is the chapter where I admit that if I have to fight with my school district over my son's education one more time, I'm gonna slice some car tires. It's where I also admit that I am scared that Nic will keep hitting and screaming when he's bigger and stronger than Al and me. That is both scary and completely my fault because I am a bad mother. And what will happen to Nic once school is over and he has to make his way in the real world? Every parent worries, but tenfold when a child has a disability. This is the chapter where I confess ('cuz he's a priest, get it?) that I don't always joyfully skip to the nursing home to see James, all Florence Nightingale-ishly, because it is so sad to see him like he is, and not be able to make it all better. And because sometimes he's really mean to me, and who needs that?

Making it all better is the whole idea for me deep down, it seems. *I* can make Nola her "old self" again, as she says, if I just try harder. *I* can turn my school district around for Nic and all the children like him who have parents who question the system, if I just try harder, and, oh boy, if I just tried harder to be a better mother, he wouldn't get so angry that he'd scream and hit like he does. *I* can get James out of the nursing home and back to work, or home to his mother's and all rehabilitated if I just try harder and talk or write to more people or make more calls – it's the only thing James wants and I can't give it to him. I don't like what I see, so *I* am going to change it, that's all.

But my mother is not her "old self" just yet, the fight goes on with school, Nic still explodes, and James will not be going home any time soon. He even seems to be getting sicker. If these are the measures I've set up for "all better," I am failing Nola, I am failing James, and I am most definitely failing Nic. It drains me to think this way. This thought makes it feel like I've done nothing to help anyone and driven myself crazy all at the same time. I realize, though, that it is partly because I've set myself up to do things for others that do not involve their free will, their ability or their desire – just mine. They are all certainly worthy goals, but they aren't my goals; they are someone else's for me to support, assuming they want these goals too. None of these goals can happen overnight for my mother, my son or my friend. Some of them may not happen at all.

So, two things: I am not so much a person who is a failure as I am a person who is fundamentally intolerant of and disappointed in her lack of superpowers. Also, I am still struggling with the fact that some changes just take so long to happen. What is the deal with that? I want changes to happen while I'm still energized so I can move on to the next challenge and solve that one too. I don't want to wear out before it's time to stop trying.

But what about the "getting there?" Obviously, I am not able to steer these metaphorical buses I'm riding on with my mother, my son or my friend. I'm just a passenger too. Is there something to be said for the paths we are on together, despite the fact that we have reached no particular destination as yet? Can't any path lead us to someplace good, toward what God intends for them, even? Toward what God intends for me? Can't God maybe drive the bus a little faster?

Can't God just move over and let me drive?

The Beatitudes in any New Testament say something along the lines of "Blessed are the poor in spirit; the kingdom of heaven is theirs." When I was a child, and up till fairly recently, I did not have much understanding or regard for that particular line of Scripture. It sounded more to me like blessed are the wimps, they shall inherit the whole enchilada, and that didn't make sense at all. Poor in spirit? Year after year, I would hear or read that line, rolling my eyes at the idea that I was supposed to be submissive to be successful. As I got older and grudgingly admitted to my lack of super powers, I finally started to understand it just a little better, to give the words a deeper listen. I think now that *blessed are the poor in spirit* might mean something to the effect that the blessing is on those who place their problems in God's hands after they've done all they can. It may place the blessing on those willing to ride the bus to where the higher power they believe in leads them. It may mean that when it's time to get off the bus, somehow problems will ultimately (perhaps not even in ways that we'll ever know) work out.

The path is not clear. The destiny is not clear. All we can be sure of is that we're riding on the path together and there is some rough terrain along this road. When people like me finish with our grieving over the changes and the challenges we see in those we love, we can begin to recognize that we do not have to lose the soul of the relationships. We may lose something, but it isn't the essence of what we had with the other person. The togetherness is always there, it just looks different now.

And perhaps what I need to be sure of is that along these paths I travel with my mother and my friend and even with Nic, there may be lots of those unexpected turns in the road, and that perhaps the best I can do is ride along and hold tightly to the people I love, for those moments when it gets really bumpy.

Two Points for Showing Up

*"Gratitude is the memory of
the heart."*
– Italian proverb

Traumatic brain injury did not take away the fact that my friend James "got a mouth on him." When we first met, I was often taken aback by his straightforwardness as well as his tendency to be quite sarcastic. Some of my fellow churchgoers did not appreciate his off-the-altar mouth when they dealt with him. Truth be told, I did not especially appreciate it either. But good little Catholic girls like me think twice before back-talking a priest, so I often felt as if I had to hold my tongue out of respect for the office if not the man.

Fortunately, I got over my restraint pretty quickly as we became more like Bronx Girl meets Philly Guy than layperson deferring to parish priest. I began to notice that when I did indeed answer back, James even backed down a bit or seemed to enjoy the element of verbal sparring that this mere curly-haired church member had dared to enter into with him. He also often responded by blushing so fiery red it must have burned his cheeks. I know it embarrassed and humbled him sometimes, this telltale face of his, but I found it endearing and revealing of his regular guy-ness. James grew on me because I started to see on his face what I did not always hear in his salty retorts.

Trying to be mindful of the effects of his illness, I find myself verbally sparring with James a bit more carefully now. As the person he was before the accident merges with the after-effects of his injuries, there's sometimes a combination of humor, fury and despair that infuses his comments with a frustrating ambiguity. I find myself asking "What do you mean by that?" (and its alternate forms: "*What* do you mean by that?" "What do you *mean* by that?" and "What do you mean by *that?*") more than I ever had to before his accident. I'm trying not to be hurt by a callous remark given in response to a simple question. I'm trying not to be shocked by an off-color comment some might correct as "inappropriate." I'm trying to understand on the fly and say something that will be mindful of who James is today, and mindful of who he isn't today. I'm also guarding my emotions a bit, because when it's hard to understand what someone means, I tend to take their words at their worst. It's definitely a perspective I need to work on, this bit of caring detachment, to keep me anchored when a storm arises.

So when James and I are "on" at the same time, it remains fun to sass him. He doesn't smile too much since his accident, so when I do see a little grin slip across his face, I share not just the moment's amusement, but this other little "Yeah!" feeling as well. It's like I'm saying, "Yeah! We did it!" 'cause for a little while, we are the way we once were, two people getting a kick out of each other. My dear friend and me. *Yeah!*

We were having an "on" moment this night, sparring just a bit about the topic of what I was supposed to bring when I came to visit. James's requests are few, and they are almost always of the edible variety. I don't know that he was particularly hungry this night, but it seemed like he had to ask anyway, for this night, I had come empty-handed.

"Got any chips?"

"No."

"Cheese steak?"

"No, James."

"Cookies?"

"I brought nothing, James."

"Why not?"

This is not always said with a smile, but tonight I knew that though pulling something out of the purse would have been gladly received, it was not that big of a deal. It was just for the sport of it that I was getting grief that night.

"Well, because I brought myself, for God's sake! I'm coming home from work. I just got off the highway, and I didn't get a chance to buy anything!"

"You could go downstairs to the cafeteria. They have vending machines."

"No."

"Why not?"

"Stop already. Don't I get at least two points for showing up?"

A pause.

"You get five."

So you know the next time the purse will be full of snacks.

I think no matter how altruistic I aspire to be, no matter how selfless I wish I were, it really is nice to hear once in a while that it matters that I'm there. Gratitude doesn't sound the same on everyone – on James, you have to almost catch it whizzing by you like a fastball – so I think it's best to be open to getting it in big ways and little ways, and enjoying it, because if you don't see it for a while again, the buzz is gonna have to last.

Acceptance is Not the Same as Resignation

"God grant me the serenity to accept the
things I cannot change,
courage to change the things I can,
and the wisdom to know the difference."
– Reinhold Niebuhr

The investigation is about to begin. Nola has taken a turn for the worse again, but this time there's a different feel to it. It's a scary, this-is-not-gonna-change-back feel for the first time.

My sister Gail and I took our mother Christmas shopping this past week. Before we left, we watched her slowly wandering around the house in search of her house keys, then her hat, then her money (not that I don't do that too). She sat motionless in the passenger seat of my car, silently gazing out the window for much of the trip (not that I don't do that too – when I'm not driving, of course). Gail and I escorted our mother through store after store in the mall and watched her staring blankly, seemingly puzzled by the huge array of greeting cards at the local Target. I do that too, but I pick a card and move on. Nola did not. I nervously realized that if Gail or I moved out of her visual field, she would surely panic.

Gail and Mike and I have seen the depression, the anxiety, the forgetfulness. We have checked medications, made schedules, filled in calendars. We have tried to jolly and to guilt her out of bed in pajamas at 4:00 in the afternoon. We have seen and felt and heard her frustration. We have been on the business end of her anger when she feels adamant that no one understands. We have tried to provide strategies for getting around tasks Nola has so much more difficulty doing now. My sister, my brother and I have all gotten the repeated phone calls asking the same question and tried to answer it, but now these calls sometimes end with her in tears. We've never seen the trifecta as bad as it's been the last few weeks, and the sibs and I are alarmed.

So we will be watching. We kind of knew that our next move of hiring a homemaker a few hours a week to help our mother with the house, the cooking and the shopping would be upsetting to her, a jolt to her pride. We joked with her that she'd be getting a maid just like she had in Jamaica when she was young (the "maid" we hired even was *from* Jamaica, as it turned out). Nola seemed to be okay with that. She *seemed* to be, but I wondered what must it feel like to have some paid stranger come in at this point in your life to do for you what you've always done for yourself and your family? Does our mother need time to adjust? Or are we in a different place now?

I ask myself, what if we can't fix this round of depression (and whatever else we're seeing0? What if we never find just the right "cocktail" of medications or never get her to take them regularly? What if she never gets used to having the help that my parents' insurance dollars paid for all those years so they could live out their lives supported in their own home when the time came? What happens when that discomfort becomes another topic for the rounds of the phone calls? Once again, I have to deal with my lack of superpowers, and I guess my sister and brother will have to as well. And we may have to accept that things are not going to change too much this time.

I look at my mother right now and I feel as if I'm seeing her through glass. It's like she can see me too but she can't hear me very well. I can see her, but her words as she calls out to me are muffled, so I have a hard time understanding what she's trying to tell me. She calls to me again and again. She's trapped inside the glass and I can't seem to get her out. There's a little opening, like a screen window, but I can't get it to open wide enough to let her out.

Perhaps I have to accept that I may have a mother who's harder to reach now through this glass and screen, but it will not stop us from trying. My sister, my brother and I may have to accept that things are different now. But accepting this change in our mother does not mean we are resigning ourselves, or her, to it. So what does it mean? What are we supposed to do now?

Serenity to accept the things I cannot change.
Courage to change the things I can.
Wisdom to know the difference.

Okay, so there's a reason people love this verse. Some don't even put the "Oh God, grant me…" part on the front, and it still makes sense. I always get the feeling that being serene about what I cannot change is like sitting all white-robed and cross-legged in a state of rapture. And since that probably won't happen, I'll have to find a little serenity by first accepting the situation as is. Maybe then I can see if it even can be changed at all.

The sibs and I can't make change if we don't jump the hurdle of saying "It looks like she is this way now," and start moving beyond that hurdle jump. I do not love this, but I cannot ignore it. Acceptance is not the same as resignation and that's the good news.

The sibs and I will be watching Nola carefully this Christmas when we all get together for dinner. But we will have to be thoughtful and reflective in deciding what, if anything, there is to do with what we find. We can still help to make change, we just need to better understand what it is we're trying to change.

And to accept what we cannot.

Are we ever going to be wise enough to know the difference?

Changes Are Not Endings

*"To everything there is a season, and
a time to every purpose under heaven. "*
– Ecclesiastes 3:1

My friend Trish and I were sitting in my office one afternoon last fall, discussing our children. Trish commented that it seems to her that we are on friendlier terms with our children than our parents were with us, and I knew what she meant. Raising my children today feels somewhat different to the way I was raised, which is not to say one way is better than the other. They are just different. Trish and I agreed that we were a lot more anxious about displeasing our parents than our children seemed to be of displeasing us. And we didn't know quite what to do about such breaches of authority like when a teenager tells you they'll get off the computer "in a while" when we tell them we want to use it now. Is it that, as the modern parent, we're supposed to give them a five-minute warning and then coordinate our needs with theirs; or tell them to get off now or else they won't use it again for a week? Trish and I were not sure and figured it was to be handled on a case-by-case basis.

From time to time, my daughter Courtney will make a remark about the way she hears some of her friends speak to their parents. One friend, she felt, was incredibly disrespectful, yelling at her mother over the phone, and screaming in fury on another occasion as the mother drove them to the mall. It made Courtney uncomfortable to be in the same place with the two of them. Another friend, my daughter commented, was always so very serious in conversation with her mother and Courtney wondered why. "You and I would have joked about that," she said to me of the topic on which the two had spoken so intensely. "We joke a lot," she said.

"And yet I manage to maintain my image as an authority figure," I answered, not sure if I was telling her or asking her.

She laughed. "How do you do that?"

I learned it from Nola. As I grew into a teenager and later a young adult, the super-strict mother of my childhood years began to loosen up, that's how. Somehow, though, Nola maintained boundaries, a certain expectation of our baseline respect in any conversation; and my sister and I pretty much adhered to it. Even in lighter moments, Nola was always ultimately the mother, not the buddy or the girlfriend, and that role definitely worked for all of us. It felt like we could still be comfortable in our roles as mother and daughters, even as the roles began to evolve to a more adult relationship. The playing field leveled a bit as we grew older, though slowly. Nola saw that we needed to make some mistakes in order for us to grow up, and that she had to watch us trip, fall and pick ourselves up without her sometimes. She began to speak to my sister and me as the young women we were becoming, rather than the children we had once been. Still, we depended on our mother to help us chart our course, and let us lean on her when we needed it.

Seeing Nola changing as she has in this last few years has made it more difficult to stay in our roles right now. I find myself feeling reluctant, sometimes even resentful, about her growing dependence on others like my siblings, my father, and assorted neighbors to do tasks for her that she formerly did for herself. I catch myself and I try to think my way out of it, but I liked my old role as daughter and I'm not eager to give it up. The situation, however, is telling me I now have to modify my idea of what it means to be the daughter.

I suppose some resistance is natural here. I have to separate myself from other people's pain a bit at first, maybe if only to try to process it in my head. I'm uncomfortable, I'm ambivalent but I want to be kind. It's as though there's my mother and there's me, very separate in these difficult moments where we weren't before. I don't understand her as

I once did. I don't know right away how to respond to a mother who is leaning on me, rather than me leaning on her. It's as though if I give her what I can I will lose something, principally the illusion that my mother is the same strong person she was when she was well. It's time to get over it, now. It's time to let go of this fear of loss that's paralyzing me. It's time to realize that I may not be able to rescue her and she probably can't rescue me the way she once could when we were both younger – and that's the way it is. It's got to be *us* now in a version of mother and daughter that speaks to this moment, not the mommy and me of my youth. I mean, lucky me, I still have a mother! It doesn't have to be about loss all the time.

When we lose the idea of being separate from one another, we don't have to measure how much giving of ourselves is too much giving. We don't have to worry about who's leaning on who. Letting go a bit can be a means to its own end, as we navigate this new "us" together. I have to be present to where she and I are right now, and when I am there, I see that the love is still there too. I'm not losing my mother, but mother and daughter are together now in a different way. We will both do better here if I can admit this shift to myself, even though I really don't like it much at all. I think my mother might do better here too if she can perhaps loosen her mental grip on the "old self" she constantly compares herself to and surrender the middle-aged Nola of the past to the now elderly Nola. Easier said by me than done by her. A new peace can only manifest when my mother and I are open to letting go of our resistance and fear. It's not the end of a relationship or an identity; it's a change. But the change does not lessen the love.

Part 6 – You Get Five Points for Showing Up

It Matters

"The right mixture of caring and not
caring – I suppose that's what love is."
– James Hilton

James told me I got five points on the night when I asked him for two points for my effort at showing up. I was taken aback by the gratitude in his response. *Being there* matters.

If I were to calculate the hours of time I've spent with my mother just since I started writing about her, the total would be in the thousands, plus a few hundred more in all those phone calls. With Nic, face-to-face, the hours would be in the tens of thousands. If I had to calculate the amount of hours I spent with James in the last three years, let's see, I'd have to multiply the number of weeks in a year times three years, times two hours a week, less vacations, but extra for time when I was there more than for once in a week... okay, that'd be a lot of time there, too.

I don't think about each and *every* one of those visits. Every hour I've spent with James, Nic, and Nola has not been a "revelation." Each evening I put Nic to bed was not an opportunity for meditating on our day – but sometimes it was. With each visit I made to my mother's house, I did not notice something transcendent and poignant in her or her struggles – but sometimes I did. Each time James got angry at me, and there had been many, I did not soldier through my hurt feelings and remember how truly brave he is for living through the turn his life took – but sometimes I did. It was those sometimes when I did notice, that I learned a bit more about how to be present. It was those times when I noticed and felt something deeply about who I was with, or where I was, or why, that I learned a bit more about how to be more supportive. It was in those moments that weren't about challenges but just about being together that I think I felt, and hopefully shared, a little joy. But I had to be there, in the room. I had to show up. Each of those thousands of hours is important just by the fact that they exist at all.

Showing up looks different from Nic to Nola to James. I live with Nic, and it's not that big of a house. Showing up for Nic really has no starting and ending point, no one particular place where it happens – being Nic's mother is a lifetime, multi-setting, eighteen-to-life commitment. Certainly Nic is everywhere in my life (especially in the kitchen when someone's making a snack). Showing up for Nic sometimes looks like countless meetings at school to create his education plan, like making phone calls so he can invite a friend over (we're still working on that), inordinate amounts of time with him in the bathroom (huh), calling the pediatrician for referrals to see one type of specialist or another, doing the soccer-mom-drive-him-everywhere thing, and sitting around watching a 12-year-old's version of good TV. Even when Nic goes to sleepaway camp for two weeks in the summer, my cell phone is on and I'm waiting for a call to say that for some reason or other his mom and dad need to go there and get him (fortunately, in three years of sleepaway summer camp, this call has yet to come). And when the day comes that Nic is ready to move out of our home to be on his own, showing up will be defined by whatever will foster success out in the world without his family in the next room waiting for his call for help.

I know that there has been a sequence and an overlapping of learning in my experience of presence to Nic first, to James and, finally, to Nola in her later years. What I've learned from one person's

160

situation I found myself applying to another's and sometimes out in the rest of the world too. I think my reflections on presence and what it means and looks like actually began with the youngest member of this trio, the one who had all the complications even before he was born. I continue to learn the value of patience and perseverance through Nic, as most parents do through their children. I continue to learn to slow down and take notice before proceeding. Some of Nic's challenges like toileting and communication have been issues far longer than they are for the typical child, so our family, even his sister, has become accustomed to a certain level of patience and perseverance, and we have adapted to a bit of the weird, the unexpected and the magical that is sometimes found in the world of disability.

This cultivation of patience came in handy when I reconnected with James after our years of estrangement. Standing outside of the bathroom waiting for him one day, I thought about how some of his personal challenges had become quite similar to Nic's. I found I could generalize and try to apply a little bit of the patience and perseverance that I continue to learn as Nic's mom in trying to be present to James, at least physically. Knowing that there were matters I had to deal with to support James (like helping him with the most intimate of personal functions), I thought about how I simply had to get over myself and the barriers in myself that I'd initially erected to supporting James as an adult, a clergyman, a non-relative, and a person I hadn't really spoken to for years. I just had to suck it up and get in there and support him with tasks he could no longer do without help, like using the toilet or brushing his teeth. At the same time, I had to be sensitive to a grown man's embarrassment over needing such intimate help from me. I had to tread carefully and respectfully as he became accustomed to my assistance, much as I need to be sensitive to Nic's embarrassment of needing my help as he gets older.

Then my mother's dementia and depression started to surface and there are times, ongoing times, when I still erect barriers to helping her. I can almost see the resistance like it's one of those detour signs where the road work hasn't begun yet and you wonder why you can't just sneak your car through and simply avoid the hassle looming before you. My biggest barrier is how I sometimes rationalize that my siblings and I really shouldn't have to do all this caregiving because, a-ha, she's the mom, after all.

It's that issue of breaking away from the idea of what we're conditioned to think we (and others) should do, of the comfort of our expected roles. But at those times I find that those barriers really have to somehow get broken down so something good can happen. That's just it, period, end of sentence. It reminds me of a phrase James used in a sermon all those years ago, don't let anybody *should* on you. There is no time – just no time – to spend being paralyzed by what was *supposed* to happen, by what *should* happen. Staying mired there is the death of possibility."

It seems to me that being present to people in their challenges is sometimes, at its most basic, simply about not being *somewhere else* instead of there with them. It is about putting my physical presence in the place where that person is, just as you are, hungry, tired, happy, sad, whatever. Sometimes that's all I bring – no wisdom, no particular attention, no pizza, just my little old self. And that's okay. Showing up still has it all over not being in the room. Being present physically will give you the opportunity, if you take it, to be there in other ways; emotionally, to laugh or cry together; mentally, to solve the big problems or rant about the little ones; and spiritually, to pray for one or both of us. It's an opportunity for me and for the person I'm with in that moment. Without me, there is no chance, no moment.

Often, with Nola, presence really is about its physical manifestation first. When Nola's feeling really low, my sister or I will get a call that asks, "Can you come over today?" A mother literally wants one of us to simply show up at her house. In those moments, it seems she just doesn't remember that I have children and a full time job and live an hour away. In those moments, perhaps she doesn't remember that Gail is easily two hours away and immersed in work. Perhaps she does remember and doesn't really care at that moment, who knows? We do our best to be there. Time and our life's obligations may not allow our response to be exactly as she wants it to be when she wants it to be, but we do respond, 'cause the eighteen-to-life commitment of family works both ways.

It's pretty subjective, this idea of presence. I think that each person in this situation has his own take. I know when I've been emotionally moved by something that happened between James or Nic or my mother and me, but do I know if they were moved by that same experience? Was my presence comforting, healing, or encouraging to them when I thought it was? Maybe it was, maybe it was not. Maybe I was reduced to tears, and they were having a yawn and a stretch. I'm betting that there were emotions and insights and responses in which I was tightly wrapped that they didn't even notice. But I'm also betting that it may have worked the other way sometimes, too – they were moved while I was the one yawning and stretching. The point then, I think, is to be available, body, mind, spirit, or some combination of these, and be open to what can happen *because you are there*.

So here are my five points for showing up:

One point for realizing that a couple hours won't kill ya, so just go for it.

The universe will let you slide if you can't always muster a couple hours, but do commit to getting there regularly, even if for a little while.

Another point when you discover that you can use the insight that you have learned here somewhere else, with someone else, or in some other situation.

A third point for the probability that this experience is making you a better person even while it sometimes drives you nuts.

Point four for realizing that you may or may not ever be recognized or thanked for doing what you're doing by this person or anyone else. You may even get yelled at, swung at, called a name or two or be totally ignored at times.

You get your fifth point for doing it anyway.

When all else fails, and I know I should but I don't wanna, I think it perhaps helps to be a little self-serving. The self-serving angle may be to show up because some day you'd prefer to be glad you did rather than sorry you didn't. I figure, let guilt work for you! It's probably not the most wholesome motivator, but on the flip side, it has been my experience that regret for what I did not do is almost impossible to shake.

I'll take it one step further: Show up and be mindful of the importance of your presence because if you weren't there, perhaps no one would be. Sometimes literally no one. Show up because you won't be there for the little miracles and surprises if you do not. Show up and be thankful that you are able to be there with your body, mind, and spirit – or at least best two out of three. You're doing a good thing.

I have read too many times that while we may regret some of the things we do, it is regret for the things we did not do that tortures us the most. I found that out for certain this year because of James.

Part 7 – Presence to Me

"How far you go in life depends on your being tender with the young, compassionate with the aged, sympathetic with the striving, and tolerant of the weak and strong. Because some day in your life you will have been all of these."
— **George Washington Carver**

The Unexpected Return of James, *Part 2*

October 27

1:30 a.m.

Dear God,

Well, James finally gets to go home. I know he was worried that he wasn't good enough and that you'd know his flaws and not forgive them, but I'm betting that you're just not like that. I'm betting that you're clothing him in sparkling white vestments as I write this, transforming his tired body to perfection, his mind to perfection, his failed heart, always beautiful, to perfection too. I know that you're welcoming him to his eternal home, the place he knew was real, the place he gave it all for.

It's been a long, tough road for my friend James. I'll miss him for the rest of my life. I got to tell him that late last night, and now begins the first day of that life. I saw him before and I saw him after. I was touched that his mom called me when it was looking like the end was near. "He had a heart attack in the nursing home," she said. And they brought him over to the hospital, but James's heart was giving out. It didn't look good.

In the space of two days, I saw him four times. Anxious now that I had to travel to Harrisburg for business on Wednesday, I only had those two days to be with him before leaving town. I couldn't take a chance that James would hold on to life until I returned. After eighteen years of friendship — especially the wonder of these last three.

On the first visit, I found James asleep in his darkened room. There I am, 7:30 a.m., just to be present, just to sing a little something, a hymn I'd heard the week before and for some reason committed to memory. Way before visiting hours, just by asking nicely and looking as miserable as I felt. The second time, a huge blessing to me, a miracle of timing. No one at the front desk to ask who I was and deny me a pass because I wasn't family. James, wide awake now; a last chance to talk. Couldn't feed him pizza tonight, just ice chips.

"I'm dying," he whispered.

What could I say to that? I- I couldn't lie and tell him he was wrong. I could see him fading in and out. His life seemed to be slipping away as we spoke, as his heart raced and his body tensed again and again. Our eyes fixed on each other in those moments, then his body relaxed for a few minutes. I could see it all in the monitor beside him — a heart attack after little heart attack, even as we spoke.

What did we say that last night? James still couldn't figure us out. It was as though I lived on some other side of him that he didn't understand. But he nodded just a bit when I reminded him not to worry about it now. It was simply that he loved me and I loved him, and that was just the way it was, my dear friend.

Enough of the mush. Some small talk now. We decided I would bring a plain pizza for that day in the future when he left the hospital. Definitely not the pepperoni he asked for the last time. I reminded him of how incredibly tough he was. I reminded James how he died three times in the ER after his car accident, but he kept reviving. Just like "A Hard Man Fe Dead," as the old Prince Buster Calypso song goes. I threatened to sing that to him when he was well again and asked him if he knew what that song title meant.

"Tough guys are hard to kill?" James guessed. — okay, James spoke Calypso.

I got the feeling now that we were truly having our last conversation. Holding myself together as best I could, I told him sadly and sincerely that there would be a hole in the rest of my life if he did die tonight. I asked him to promise me that he'd come back to me and let me know he was okay. I couldn't continue to act as he was not going to pass on very soon.

The third visit I felt such tightness in my chest, probably this morning's upper body over-exertion on exercise TV maybe. Or maybe reminders of the pain of another, of my dear friend, since I couldn't exercise that thought away. A strange connection to make, if only in my head. Maybe just an incredible sadness and an anticipation of the worst, aching for release. Watching my evening grad class leave early — *they* were done with tonight's project, after all — *and* walking out the door behind them instead of stalling them because the class technically wasn't really over yet. Then James's sister calling me in my car on the way home with the news that James had a massive heart attack some time last night after I'd gone home. He was not going to last this night. I should come now, if I want to.

I want to.

I wonder if I really was the last person he spoke to in this life. Why me?

I enter a hospital room crammed with some of James's brothers, their wives, a nephew. It seems everyone knows who I am. "Oh, it's Jimmy's friend Gerry," they whispered to each other after greeting me warmly. I wonder how they know who I am. Whatever, it's nice. Everyone's chatting... brothers and their wives, a nephew. Me, so awkward with strangers, especially when the guest of honor is in the bed with only morphine for his pain and they've turned off the monitors.

They've turned off the monitors.

Is anyone going to cry or break out a rosary or something? I'm realizing that our presence is our prayer — perhaps it's too hard to be that formal right now. I suppose it's the kind of stuff priests take care of when you call for them at moments like this. I gaze at James, his heaving chest, listening to his breath stop just a bit too long, then start again, then stop once more. I notice James's eyelids flutter as I lean toward him and say, "Hello." Is he with us... a little? Does he know it's me?

It feels cold in this room, despite all the people.

WWND?

I try to go with the flow. I try to converse casually with nice people I barely know. I'm so bad at small talk that I mostly hang back and listen. I hear lovely and amusing stories about how generous James was with his family, his friends, people he barely knew, and I smile. James would give you the shirt off his back without a thought. And never once did I get to treat him to lunch.

I think back to 1999, and a call I made on New Year's Eve at about 10:00 p.m., even later than it is now. My infant, Nic, lying in Bryn Mawr Hospital in an oxygen tent, so very sick. Was he going to make it through the night? I'm thinking like a Catholic now; I need a priest to administer the sacrament of the sick, which is a blessing to the gravely ill. I make a call. "James, if you get some time, can you come and anoint Nic soon?"

James was kind of literal sometimes. He left the people he was with that New Year's Eve, and was in Nic's room an hour later, because James was a generous man.

One of his brothers and his wife has to leave now. Another brother plans to spend the night. He's getting ready to get his wife home too, but says he'll be right back to keep vigil. I say my good nights. People I hardly know hug me, it's like that tonight. I touch James one last time, passing my hand over his hair, then resting it lightly on his arm one last time. He is cold as ice and clammy to the touch. I ache with sadness as I drag myself to the elevator. I'm phoning Al as I leave the room to let him know I'm on my way home. Visiting hours are over now and you can't get in the building anymore. As I walk down the ramp a man is looking up at me smiling in an almost familiar way. As I near the door I tell Al I'll talk to him later, because I see that I have to let another of James's brothers into the hospital.

"Are you one of James's brothers? I'm Gerry."

"Yes, I know."

He and I have another connection, though, and we talk about our sons with disabilities; his with autism, and my Nic. We hug too. It's like that tonight.

I can't hold it together now, I lose my last bit of composure walking to the car. I'm crying all the way home, hoping there are no cops to pull over the sobbing woman in the little black car.

Hugs from my Courtney and Al when I get home. It helps. I call Gail, it helps. Everyone reminds me I did so much for James. I hope James knows he did so much for me.

I drag myself up the stairs to my bedroom, but the phone rings before I can flop on to my bed. Reading the caller ID, Al whispers, "It's for you."

James has passed.

Now what?

"Would it be weird if...?"

The three voices confirm my heart's desire.

"Go back," says Gail.

"Go back," says Al.

Even Courtney knows, I have to go back.

James's brother stands alone gazing at James. Yellowed and motionless. James appears almost waxy in the fluorescent light that baths his lifeless body. I cross over to the other side and sit by his bed. I nervously rest my fingertips on the hand of my first dead person. No longer cold and clammy, James simply feels still. He is one with the temperature of the room, neither warm like the living nor icy cold like he felt before I left. To my surprise, I feel a cool white energy shoot up my arm, across my shoulders and down the other arm, out my other hand. I stiffen, my glance darting to his face.

What was that?

Another brother returns, his vigil over before it started.

A few minutes later, James's mother arrives. Her delicate frame supported by a cane now as she says only "I've run out of tears," and sits down by her baby, her firstborn, her darling forever.

"My poor Jimmy," she sighs.

Brother Joe is there now. Day after day, Joe and Mom were always there.

James's sister returns. She wipes James's brow gently, then remarks, "You know what he'd say if he was alive? 'Too close'."

She'd broken the somber mood of the moment. We have to smile.

I kneel by James's dear mother. She's realizing that this is how it had to be. The home James needed to go to was not of this Earth. She holds his hand and beholds her son.

The silence passes. A new conversation begins at the far edge of the bed.

"Wait, funeral arrangements. Where, that parlor in Springfield?"

"Didn't Jimmy know the owner?"

"Yeah, but the owner died this year... maybe we can call ... "

Well, I know it's time for me to go now. I always had a hard time leaving James. My husband and sister-in-law call my inability to part company quickly a family trait, the "Anderson goodbye". How do you leave someone to the life he had these last three years? Parting words return to my memory.

"One more sip of water? Sure."

"Do you really need me to take you to the bathroom again? All right, but then I really have to go, James, really."

I root around in my purse to pull out a piece of paper I'd been carrying since Sunday. A hymn I had never heard till last week, although it's as old as anything. "Precious Lord, take my hand, lead me on, let me stand... I am tired, I am weak, I am worn... through the storm, through the night, lead me on to the light... take my hand, precious Lord, lead me home." The same hymn I sang to James as we sat alone at 7:30 in the morning the day before.

I ask if anyone would be interested in perhaps singing together now before I go. I tell them the name of the song. No one knows the hymn, but they like the idea of a moment of reflection at James's deathbed.

Yikes. So, now it's a solo. So not "me". I imagine James sitting on a cloud having a cigarette and a chuckle at my expense.

I fumble through my purse for my now essential reading glasses, but damn it, no glasses in the case. I can't see the small type and I don't know the words by heart. Embarrassed, I prepared to take back my offer, but at once, I remember the nursing home. I ask, "Are James's glasses here?" I learned, when cleaning them off for him after a haircut, that I could see just fine through them, and had borrowed them once or twice back in his room.

So, in this moment, it's like, "Heh, stop laughing and pass the glasses, Jim, I need your help."

I can focus on the lyrics now, and I do my best. I hit almost all the notes.

My audience thanks me. "I'll take that," James's sister says as she pockets the paper with the song lyrics.

It's really time for me to leave now. I have to go home too.

In gratitude, sadness and maybe just a little bit of peace,

Gerry

My Turn?

"But all endings are beginnings. We
just don't know it at the time."
– Mitch Album

Seven years of friendship, seven years of estrangement, then three years – almost four – deeply reconnected. I never expected to see James again after all the years we spent apart, but it's the way life happens, I guess. Our reconnection through the small persistent voice that told me to find him again. The shock of finally finding him so very desperately ill, sentenced to congregate care long before his time. A reconnection only strengthened by the hours in the nursing home week after week, year after year, to rehab, to intensive care, to the death bed, to the grave. Who knew?

I stepped out into the warmer-than-usual October night and pulled my cellphone from my bag. Funny how when a person passes, it feels like you just have to call someone to tell them. So, I called my friend Kate. She worked with James at the parish too, long ago. It felt okay to hear myself speak the words. It felt bad to have to say them. She said I was a saint again. Still incorrect. We hung up, and I climbed into my car.

James's passing was not really part of my plan, no matter how much I noticed his decline in the last few months. My heart just ached, of course, but not really from a sense of surprise at the occurrence that was his passing. I worried that James was different after the skin cancer operation at the end of the summer; he had seemed almost hollowed out by it after the surgery, just worn all the way down. I began to wonder how much longer his suffering would go on. I wondered what would be left of his life in a year. I wondered if I would make it to the finish line with him, and now it seemed that I had. I took my time driving home that night, just to think, to be enveloped in the darkness of this midnight hour. No tears welled in my eyes on the way home. This time, I just drove.

James's passing was so much more than sad to me. Sad did not seem the correct word, so my thoughts began to lead me elsewhere. Perhaps this loss was also a moment for awe of the invisible bridge between life and death. My dear friend had only been deceased for an hour. Where was he now? Was he really gone?

In a small way, I also felt a sense of release. I mean, how could I not feel just a little bit relieved, despite my sorrow? Was that honest or cruel? The man was out of that broken body, that wounded brain, that tired heart. Was James now at the start of the promise of *resurrection*, the *eternal reward*, all that good stuff to which he had dedicated his life? Was he now enjoying the fruits of his faith, the faith he never surrendered in the agony of confinement to a nursing home? I knew he had not; I often asked him about his faith as we sat together. At his bedside in the evening, I sometimes queried whether he still believed, whether he still felt God was with him in all his suffering. The answer was always yes. It wasn't always yes with an exclamation point, though. In the moments where he wondered why all of this happened to him, I wondered with him. Sometimes we would begin to say a rosary together, even though we didn't often finish. James was always willing to pray with me.

Once in a while I would ask for his blessing before I left him for the night. I would often receive sincere but playful little signs of the cross all over my face followed by a smack on the cheek; I was glad James and God still had a sense of humor. So in death, the Dallas Cowboys fan reached the goalpost, the Phillies fan hits home plate. The pain was over. In his last months, I often asked God why he didn't just take James already. And then when he did take him, I'm a little bummed.

I spent much of the week between James's death and his funeral on the road for my job. I had been granted the wish to be able to say goodbye before I left for Harrisburg, and now it was time to start my trip west. My thoughts of James surfaced constantly, perhaps all the more so because I didn't seem to be able to make time to just sit down and feel sad, one more good wail to let it all out. My thoughts on the road to Harrisburg would be with home, sad, and worried thoughts of my family and James'. I traveled west that next day for a conference, my grief and me, the loss of my friend, my constant companion, on the two-hour drive.

Wednesday morning began with more goodbyes, just little ones to my Al and the kids, and last-minute packing. I charged my new MP3 player, the one Gail had given me just weeks before, so that I could take some music along to play in my hotel room. She jammed it with well over 500 of our mutual favorite songs and I looked forward to hours of good listening. I fumbled with the device, testing the charge that morning before I left, by pulling up a random song on the "shuffle" setting.

The song it came up with – "A Hard Man Fe Dead". I chuckled as I remembered that this was the Calypso tune I told James I'd sing to him when he left the hospital. What a coincidence. I tried to advance to the next tune three times, but the player wouldn't budge.

The experience of James's passing played again and again in my mind. The last moments together at the hospital, this loss still only hours old. I found myself chatting aloud to him along the way in the car. I found that this monologue was comforting to me. You can say anything you want in a car by yourself, so I did. Other motorists might see you and think you're on your phone – hands-free, of course – but I was talking James's ear off.

When I arrived at the hotel, a somewhat weathered chain operation in what looked like east of nowhere, I was given a key to my room, 247. I remembered noticing the number of James's room, 274, back at the hospital. I knew when I got back that I had to play that number, boxed like Nola would do it so that I could win either way. (As it was, I lost. I thought that was a coincidence, in a numerological kind of way, although it would have been a better coincidence if I had won.)

I was handed the usual bag of agendas and handouts as I signed into the conference. As expected, there were lots of presentations to attend and some drew my attention right away. I knew I could easily lose myself in college professor world and turn down the mourning songs in my head, at least for a day or two. For the first session, I chose a presentation on the stresses of student teaching, something I'm very involved with, either being the cause or the solution, depending on the student I'm supervising. I parked myself in the back of the room, in case I needed to sneak out, but the topic held my interest as she began to talk.

The presenter spoke enthusiastically about her extensive research on the topic, her pride in the accomplishment obvious. Chatting away, she seemed to forget the slide presentation she had prepared to accompany her words. Amused, my attention shifted to the blank screen, waiting for this missing element of words and graphics to appear, fond as I am of these types of visuals.

As the presenter began to wind down her talk, she turned to her slideshow at last, asking herself aloud if there was anything she'd forgotten to say as she clicked quickly through screen after screen of text. A slide came up that said, *"Don't let anybody 'should' on you.,"* the line from one of my favorite sermons of James's so many years ago. Since when uttered quickly enough, *"Don't let anybody 'should' on you,"* sounded a bit obscene, it got the attention of the congregation back then, certainly of this member anyway. And the phrase never left me, because I thought it was true as well as clever, but I had never heard it or read it anywhere since he said it. Who knew he hadn't made it up?

What a coincidence.

Seated at the lunch table after the morning's presentation, I pulled out the handouts from the talk I had just attended so that I could share them with my colleagues. Distracted as I was by the previous "Don't let anybody should on you" slide I really enjoyed the presenter's work. Squinting at the printed word now, I realized I had not looked for my reading glasses after missing them from their case back in James's room at the hospital the night before. I had come to Harrisburg without my glasses, which promised to be a big problem for small print and me. Frustrated by my carelessness, I dug through my purse and finally grabbed my empty glass case to take a wishful look inside. And upon opening it, I found my glasses were now in the case, as they were supposed to have been last night.

What a coincidence.

My stay in Harrisburg never made it past the second day. The coincidences, as well as the educational teacher stuff, derailed before lunch was over. Checking phone messages, I found I had missed a phone call from my brother Mike as my colleagues and I finished our desserts. He left a message to let me know that our father had a heart attack. It was our dad's second this year. The conference was over for me.

I said a hasty goodbye to my lunch mates after telling them my news, and dashed to my hotel room. I shoved my belongings into my bag and walked quickly to my car to begin the long ride home.

On the road sooner than I had planned, I was now thinking and worrying about my dad as I approached the turnpike. A second heart attack. Heart problems didn't run in the family, and now a second heart attack. More damage? How much damage?

Talking to myself wasn't helping, so I started talking to James again. We certainly had a new topic for this leg of the journey. I asked him, now that he was in a better position to help, to start praying with me that my dad would recover from this second heart attack.

There's not much to differentiate the stretches of highway from Harrisburg, to Hershey to Lancaster to my exit in Downingtown; acres of rolling farmland, dairy signs to the left and right, and plenty of blue sky. As I lifted up the prayers that were all I could do for my father in this moment when I knew so little about what was going on with him, my eyes were drawn to a sign along the side of the road. The sign board outside of a small church read, *"Jesus said man should pray and not lose heart."* Okay, sign, I pray that my dad won't lose *his* heart and that my family and I won't lose heart either.

What a coincidence.

The silence around me and the tension inside me needed to be broken now. I cranked up the satellite radio to my favorite station. It plays a most eclectic assortment of songs that are current along with songs that used to be hot and songs that are just interesting surprises. I like to escape into this station on long car rides, letting my mind enjoy the rhythms and the lyrics, often letting my inner diva out for a little sing-along.

The first song I heard was familiar, but in my solitude with only meandering highway before me, I was free to really listen to the words. They spoke of how there would always be a mountain and I'd always want to move it. But the song said that what mattered was not the mountain, but the experience of climbing it.

I recognized this tune. It was Miley Cyrus singing "The Climb." It was a song that I sung along with on many a work day, but I found myself moved by the lyrics as I had not been before. The words rang so true, especially in these last few days of what felt like one really bad event after another. There was going to be more caregiving to do when I arrived home.

How would I be able to help my dad and mom, and take care of my own little family too? What about work?

Where was my dad?

How is my mom doing in all of this?

And, of course, there was a funeral to attend on Saturday.

The first song segued into another. I knew this song well: "Rockabye," in which Shawn Mullins sings a lullaby to a sad girl to let her know that everything will be alright.

A church sign, a song about life's uphill battles, a song saying that everything would be all right, the "Hard Man Fe Dead" song on the MP3 player before I left, James's line about not letting anybody *should* on you in the conference presenter's slide show, and the reappearance of my glasses to their case at lunch. Coincidence did not seem to be the right word for what was happening when I realized how many coincidences were happening in this short space of time since James's passing. I began to sense that perhaps this string of occurrences were not *coincidences* at all. Linking one to another in a span of less than 48 hours, I could no longer dismiss all of these continuous, gently meaningful and encouraging happenings as mere chance. There was a better word for it. I was experiencing *synchronicity*, an intentional alignment of events. I smiled and said aloud, "Hey, *Dear*, you trying to tell me something?"

A third song began. It was Natasha Bedingfield singing "These

Words." I had never heard this tune before. It had a dance beat and a joyful voice that sang that there was nothing else left to say but "I love you, I love you, I love you."

I began sensing a communication here now perhaps a lifting of some veil between James's new world and mine. I'd often ended my visits with James by calling out, "Love you," as I went out the door, and though I sometimes heard the words in turn, the alternate response on bad days was more along the lines of, "Yeah, you're nuts," or sullen silence. In this moment, alone in my car on the turnpike, I began to understand that this chain of songs and events... mm, wasn't random. These songs and events were connecting me to James when I so needed a comforting presence with me.

I let out a loud sob from somewhere deep, the sob that had been building for days, the one I knew I needed to have more than ever now that my dad was sick and my friend was gone...

...or so I thought.

James never liked to see me cry. I think that perhaps the song that followed was, dare I say, selected to calm me down a little, perhaps to make me laugh. It was Train singing "Hey, Soul Sister," and it reminded me of James's awkward affinity for a dress I used to wear in church sometimes when I was younger and thinner and a bit more fashion conscious. It was a slim-fitting red cocktail length dress with a wide belt that cinched my waist and gave me curves I didn't even have without it. Even in the nursing home, brain injury and all, my dear James still remembered and joked about his reaction to that dress. The song said it just wasn't fair for a girl to move like that and that the singer would always wanna blow this girls' mind.

Well, mind blown, all right. But I calmed down, and I laughed when I heard that song. The red linen dress was a memory that had always amused and embarrassed us both. But I turned off the radio at this point, realizing the immediate truth of another line in the song where the singer said he'd always want to surprise the person in the song. I was, in the moment, overwhelmed by the unfolding of all these words, in sign and in song. My already frazzled mind was now most certainly quite surprised.

In the next moments, however, it was not my mind but my bladder that began to consume my thoughts; I really needed to find a rest stop! Since the next area was 36 miles away and I am female, this meant focusing exclusively on bottling up both body and mind. So I bounced in my seat. I laughed a little, bounced some more, cried a little as I drove east just a little too fast and hoped there would be no traffic jams ahead. It was the longest half hour of my day.

I made a mad dash for the ladies room as soon as I got to a rest stop – it was now a beautiful oasis in the desert before me. As I raced through the door, I heard the stereo above me playing that same "Rockabye" song I heard in the car when Shawn Mullins told his girl that everything would be all right.

Synchronicity had followed me into the ladies' room. I'd spent a lot of time with James in the bathroom these last three years. Maybe this was poetic justice – 'cause now James was coming to the restroom with me.

Anyway, everything was all right in the end. My dad went in for his heart surgery the next day. Simple. Out in two days.

But sitting in the pre-op room with our father, praying for his recovery, Gail, Mike and I watched our dad's TV broadcasting the usual noon-time soap operas suddenly switch to a televised Mass when the orderly came in to take our father to the operating room.

What synchronicity.

Presence Revisited:
Choosing to Believe
and Receive Comfort

"We can testify to something only in the measure that we have shared in it."
– St. Thomas Aquinas

During my years of lost contact with James, I sometimes thought about how awful it would be if I had learned of his death through an announcement at church some Sunday. I imagined a priest reciting the names of the departed as they do, and the imploding atom bomb feeling I would get in my stomach upon hearing my friend's name among the clergy memorialized. If this morbid thought came to when James was alive, I would pay special attention to those announcements, and feel a little relief that another week had passed without hearing his name. James never enjoyed robust good health in all the time I knew him. He had bouts of skin cancer, battled with his weight as I do, along with several complications that I did not. Al and I once secretly clocked James smoking at the rate of one cigarette every 20 minutes at our house, so I was concerned for his well-being even before the accident. As it turned out, I actually missed Mass the weekend after he'd died, so I never got to hear the dreaded announcement of his name. Of course, by then, the announcement would've been heard as a confirmation, not a shock. So much had changed.

Despite gratitude for never having to be publicly shocked by news of James passing or from some outside source or to regret that we'd never renewed our friendship, I would've given all of the last three years that I spent with him back and taken my chances with the announcements if it could've made him well instead. Of course, life doesn't work that way. No bartering for someone's life no matter how good of an idea I think I have for the trade. As long as there's no bartering, I'm grateful for the intuitive shoves that persisted until I allowed them to lead me into that nursing home to become reacquainted with the man who awaited me there. I am blessed that James and I were given the opportunity to find each other again, to be at peace with the past and spend time together in the last years of his mortal life. Would our lives have been different if we hadn't lost contact with each other? Sure. But I will never know, and I'm trying really hard to stop wondering. But I still think about it once in a while. As long as our paths got the chance to cross again after so much time, I feel honored, touched, privileged, humbled and very, very blessed to have reconnected and been able to be present to my dear friend in his later years.

I think of the term *compassionate presence* as a way of being with another that tries to offer support, comfort, love and encouragement while being sensitive to what the person is going through, as much as I can understand it. I witness presence as my son brings me those little drinks of water when I wake up in the morning or as Nic puts his hand to my forehead to check my temperature when I'm feeling sick. I realize as I look back on my life with Nola that there will probably be never be anyone as interested in me as my mother, no one so willing to be present to my life's ups and downs. I have been the recipient of the loving presence of others all my life. But now I have a new question about this definition: Is this presence something that can only happen between the living? Can we be present to one another beyond this mortal life? I had not expected what happened after James passed on. I find that it ties together in ways that are like synchronicity!

I took James's death hard in the beginning, no surprise there. I have been blessed with a life in which I have lived almost half a century and have only been touched by the death of someone very close to me a handful of times. For example, both of my parents are still alive. I can't say I know many people my age who still have both their mother and father. I almost feel naïve about death and mourning sometimes. I'm a death virgin!

I was not particularly taken aback or repulsed or frightened by

James's stilled body in the moments after his death. I did not spend an inordinate amount of time pondering his corpse laid out in the casket at church, but I was surprised and very moved by the sense that James, in spirit, was present to me almost immediately after his death. Same definition of *present* that I used before – being with me to offer support, comfort, love, encouragement, while being sensitive to what I was going through as much as he could understand it. In those first moments beholding my dear friend as he lay at rest and placing my hand on his, I remember a cool, white streak of energy pass from his hand and up my arm. In my search for an answer to what happened that night, I was told by a hospice worker that chances are James's spirit energy was making itself known to me. She said it was not uncommon! In that first week after he passed, I experienced many little "presences" that gave me peace, both as a way of feeling he was gone from me in body only, and as a way of knowing that he was sending his support to me now. And every now and then, if I talk to him while I'm driving in my car or hear a song that makes me think of him, I know that in some way, his presence remains with me.

Still wish he was alive and well though.

"Leave the Gun, Take the Cannoli"

*"It is not as important that we are
daughters or sons or parents but
people in new caring relationships."*
– Ram Dass

It's taken about four months for the sense of James's close spiritual presence to me to become kind of second nature, more and more just another element of my life. Will this feeling of presence last? I hope so. Sometimes I recognize clear synchronicity, and sometimes I just wonder. But as I look behind me and see our metaphorical footprints in the distance, I realize that two people walking side-by-side don't have to speak to one another all the time to still be walking together.

Meanwhile, the little and large struggles and joys of presence to Nic and Nola continue. Although one man's struggles ended forever, I'm grateful that my life as mother, wife, friend, caregiver and everything else does, indeed, go on anyway. Still, sometimes I find that as my life and its challenges continue, I miss something that my visits to James provided me, escape! Stopping by the nursing home late at night, in the dark and quiet of the evening, was sometimes just a bit relaxing for me, I have to admit. No matter how I found James on a given night, what I could always be sure of was the quiet, the lull before the storm of stress I just left at work or the one that might await me at home. And I wonder if he knew how much the opportunity to just sit around and watch TV and eat junk food with a friend helped me, and how I miss it. I'm in search of new little escapes like the ones I lost with James. I still have some people to take care of.

It often occurred to me in these last few months that James's passing and all of the emotions and synchronicities since, might be there to strengthen me for what is to come. The emotions, sometimes raw, sometimes overwhelming me with a sense of presence and the happenings, so welcome and so surprising, have perhaps been there to remind me of the communion of the saints always praying for and with me, James being one of them now. For that matter, perhaps the painful and the joyful emotions and events that make up my time with Nic and Nola will continue to teach me in whatever time I get in the next decades. I'm so fortunate to have the life I have, even when things are difficult. I'm gradually coming to peace with the idea that life will not always go my way, and I still hate that fact pretty fiercely. Ultimately, though, acceptance of this fact can open me to possibility, and help me better understand my reality such as it is.

I still wrestle constantly with the "should-ing" on myself about Nola and Nic because I don't always feel that great about them or how their challenges impact my life. I still feel guilty because I fear that sometimes a good bit of resentment lurks below the surface of my efforts at kindness. Is that unkind or just to be dealt with? Is the presence always compassionate? I feel guilty in the moments where I realize that my very primal resentment I sometimes feel is of my own mother and my own child. I shouldn't feel that way but sometimes I do. As I say that, am I "should-ing" on myself? What is there to do? I have to acknowledge these ugly emotions, and I do. I still have my "select few" to talk to, and I do. I always have this communion of saints that has lately revealed itself to me, and I ask the departed to pray for me and with me.

I don't have too much time to stomp and pout; I have children to raise, parents to support, a paycheck to earn, plans to make, and pizza to eat with friends and family.

Acknowledging the ugly feelings allows me the option of letting them go – can't get rid of them if I won't admit they are there. And they're okay to have, just not to cling to. My anger and frustration will return like weeds in my garden or lost weight to my scale if I am not vigilant in acknowledging their existence and working on keeping them away. In my experience, the longer I can let go of my anger and frustration, leaving my junk at the door or dropping it off on the way out, the longer it takes them to return. And go figure, through it all, life does not stop or even slow down. Sometimes when I feel triumphant for a moment where I succeeded in letting go, I borrow the words of Julian of Norwich like a chant in my head:

"All will be well, and all will be well, and all matter of things shall be well."

They will, won't they?

Maybe not in my preferred timeframe, but I do believe all will be well. We are only here for a short while, some of us shorter than others. What harm could there be in keeping that fact before me as I live out my days? What good could there be in believing that my life is unfolding as it was meant to and that *all will be well, and all will be well, and all matter of things shall be well?*

Presence to Me:
Nola, Nic, and Life as
We Know It

"The most precious gift we can give others is our presence. When mindfulness embraces those we love, they will bloom like flowers. "
-- Thich Nhat Hanh

Premise number one: I cannot completely take away another person's struggles. Premise number two: I can try to support loved ones in their struggles if they'd like me to do so. Premise three is that between the first two, there is often a lot of work to do. The good news is that I can probably do at least some of this work of *compassionate presence* and, sometimes, even help things move in the direction they need to for another person. The better news seems to be that I sleep more soundly when I know I've at least tried to do my best for my loved ones.

Nic had a great evaluation at school last month. Al and I sat down with his team of teachers and therapists and talked and planned. We committed to his learning goals, objectives and supports to paper, and sent that beautiful document around the table for signatures of agreement. I wanted to pinch myself to see if this positive experience was a dream. No evaluation ever went as smoothly before, and we were cautiously ecstatic, if that's possible. Nic has a great teacher. He has friends. His health is, for the moment, under control. Lots of challenges and obstacles remain, but after that meeting Al and I forced ourselves to take some time to savor a moment of success and do a little happy dance.

When I think about how Nic is becoming a teenager this year, I realize that as slowly as the time has moved with him and for him, it is also blowing by like dry leaves on a blustery day. Nic will not be a child forever. I recently noticed his coarsening leg hair and the darkening above his upper lip that Al refers to as the "Spanish boy mustache." Good Lord. Do I dare to see Nic someday leaving us, moving out into the world without his mother and father holding his hands? I have to. Do I dare see him as an adult, someday even doing for me when I need from him? I have to. How do I support Nic in the achievement of his goals so that I won't have to support him because he lacked goals? This is the ongoing challenge: Al and Nic and I have so many meetings left to attend.

And while I'm thinking about Nic's future as well as Courtney's, I've still got to look at this day and this moment, because these days and moments are what will set the stage for what is to come, and, the time all runs together in the end. I still struggle to understand this young man whose spoken words are difficult to decipher, this child whose frustration so easily turns to aggression and rage, but whose killer charm and warmth make him too completely forgivable.

They say in one of the songs that I heard after James passed that life is a climb up a mountain but it's the climb itself that matters more. Hopefully along the way I'm picking up some skills and experience that will make me a better climber. What I've learned these last three years will guide my whole life going forward, not just my experiences of three people I love.

I got to try my climbing skills out on a new piece of rocky terrain a few weeks ago.

My daughter Courtney sustained a concussion from a bus accident in January of her freshman year of high school -- her first semester, no less. She, who was always the "easy" child by comparison to Nic, suddenly took center stage, missing more than two months of school under a neurologist's orders. There's something familiar here in the sudden alteration of health status, and it's terrifying upon first consideration because of the experience I already have with changes in the status of someone's brain. It is terrifying because my darling daughter is not passing the little cognitive, "Count backwards by fours, honey," testing the doctor gives her. I find myself playing a dreadful game of "What if?" before I compose myself for each step of this scary new climb. I cannot make Courtney better by sheer force of will. I couldn't do it for James or Nola, either; I'm still lacking those superpowers. The only thing I can do definitely and faithfully is to be present to her, to take her for evaluations and doctor's appointments, to make sure she's getting a lot of water, a lot of rest and not a lot of computer time as her brain slowly heals. How do you get a 15-year-old girl to stop text messaging and quiet down enough to follow doctor's orders and rest her brain? Write me with any ideas. How do you get a child caught up with school work when she has missed an entire semester? It's time to make some phone calls and to take that special education knowledge I have gained through education and experience to get supports for someone who will hopefully only be disabled for the short term.

Most importantly, in all this upheaval of Courtney's young life, I can only try to keep her spirits up and her life as close to normal as possible as we navigate her eventual return to school and watch for the possible residual effect of a blow to the head. I can only pray, pray for her and with her, but prayer has power. And let's not forget the power of the written word on the borrowed laptop to get a few things straightened out with the insurance company and the school as we work toward her return to life as she knew it. And, of course, lots of hugs, applied liberally and frequently.

I just know James is present to her in spirit on this part of her climb up the mountain. Head injury in an auto accident: He's been there.

I cannot end Nola's struggles, but the possibilities remain in presence. Once in a while, I am taken aback by the fact that my parents, who now seem so fragile and vulnerable, were smarter than any of their children about finance. Perhaps it is a trait of their generation. On the Nola front, my parents wisely bought something called long-term care insurance when they moved from the Bronx to New Jersey and had enough money to need a financial planner to help them put their funds in all the right places. My envy of their finances aside, long-term care insurance is supposed to allow elderly folk to have different types of support paid for as they need it so they can stay in their homes as long as possible. I like the idea of my folks having choices even more after these last three years of visiting a nursing home every week.

After my mother's health problems last summer, when the sibs and I decided to see if we could access my parents' policy to get her some supports, we found our Jamaican dynamo home-maker. When someone besides my self-motivated but very quiet father is around the house and my mother can alternately boss them around and joke with them, she's a different person. She's a charmer once again. It's almost as good as a visit from one of her children, if her children would clean and cook for her, too. On a good day, I almost feel like I can tell my mother my little successes and problems the way I once did, but since Nola's never stopped being a worrier, I'm cautious.

Nola always inquired about James, who she referred to as "Father Catholic" because she couldn't remember his name, and she was saddened to know of his passing. She enjoys the occasional story of my experience of synchronicity from James, as Nola has always been a believer in such occurrences. I realize with a touch of wistfulness that there is probably no one as fascinated by a child as their mother is. I miss that feeling of deep interest when Nola forgets the little things about my life that I do share with her, but I still cherish the times when we sit together and talk. I still have a mom.

These days, my mother's depression has the upper hand once again. I feel resistance building in me, wanting Nola's "old self" back again, the one I tell her she still is on those good days. This sad, scared, frustrated mother, however, is my mother, too. This woman who does not want to get out of bed most days is still Nola. I'm learning to let her be whoever she is on a given day, but sometimes I still want my "Mu". Sometimes I still want to be Nola's little girl, and have my mom there with me to take some of the weight of the world off my shoulders, but I am grateful that I have my mother, no matter how present or distant. The sibs and I are doing our best to be present to Nola.

I continue to learn day by day to share what I know and who I am to help as best I can. I try to be present – to offer support, comfort, love and encouragement while being sensitive to what Nola, Nic, and now my Courtney are going through as much as I can understand it.

Could my spin on presence make me a better person in the end? That would be great. Maybe I will notice a newfound ease with being present when responding to some new situation in which I am asked to "show up". Maybe an ease with being present will show itself when I am comfortable knowing I've done my best whether or not anyone else notices. Maybe presence is about learning to give with less worry about get.

Maybe I even learned more about presence because I wrote so much down as I lived through it. Because I so often put my thoughts on paper, perhaps I saw life with James, Nic, and Nola as I wouldn't have been able to see it in my memories alone. In my experience as two children's mother and one woman's child I continue to learn how being a parent gives you many things to talk about, laugh about, and definitely to worry about. It can also give you something to write about if you are so inclined. I still have a lot of pages to fill in my ever-present little spiral notebook.

What my mother taught me is so much of who I am and who I am becoming as this 50th birthday approaches. I use Nola's lessons as a mother myself, and my children, too, have shaped me. But when Nola's lessons started to apply to others in my world, like a prematurely gray Irish priest, I knew there was even more to discover. And so I'm learning about being there for others in a compassionate way, maybe being a little kinder to myself too. I'm learning to be open to what can happen when you do show up, and to realize that sometimes it's okay – and even necessary – to do like the story says and let go of *Italy* so you can learn your way around *Holland*.

Thank you James; thank you Nic, and you too, Courtney.

And thank you to you, Nola, my first teacher, my first advocate, my first friend. All, I believe, will be well.

But I'm going to end for now. The phone is ringing.

Epilogue

What Would Nola Say?

March 2018.

We all tried to wear blue to my mother Nola's funeral, as blue was her favorite color. I didn't really wear as much blue as I was supposed to, I remember. But the planning of the service, decorating the funeral parlor again – more on that later – and being in a bit of a daze because you never really believe your mother is going to die, made it harder than it should have to find the time and attention span to buy a pair of blue dress pants. That's a little pathetic. My blouse, however -- white with tiny blue flowers – reminded me of the type of fabric Nola liked, and so it would have to be blue enough.

My daughter, Courtney, wore navy blue – the dress blues of a sailor. And she tucked her left uniform sleeve down to cover her wedding ring. Only the innermost circle of our family knew Courtney had eloped the month before. Most of us were still digesting that she had joined the Navy last year, so elopement elevated digesting this news to heartburn, gas and bloating – at least for me, at least for a while. Her six years in the Navy would cause me endless worry, but tremendous pride as well.

I don't remember, as much as I probably should, about what Nic was doing on the day of my mother's funeral. I guess Nic was quietly hanging out in the chapel with his beloved Aunt Gail, my sister, who was probably quietly hanging out with him. Nic's favorite aunt always indulges his stories, perhaps parsing out that he was excited about trying out new jobs in the community in hopes of finding a good one after high school. Nic probably wouldn't ask Gail about her storied career in graphic design, or her many awards, but someone at the service certainly would.

Or perhaps Aunt Gail, Courtney and Nic were circulating, greeting family and friends who were paying their respects to Nola. Cousins we hadn't seen in years, but would soon see again at the funerals of their own parents – the steady, dependable aunts and uncles I think of along with my parents as "the greatest generation." But I don't remember. I just don't.

There would be food, of course. I do recall thinking that Nola would have been pleased that there was so much lunch for the guests and that we did not cook any of it. Nola felt that guests must be fed, but never insisted that the meal be homemade. She would have been amused that the funeral parlor owners graciously allowed us to cater a meal in their parlor great room as her porcelain urn, surrounded by floral sprays and a basket of sympathy cards, were posed in the adjoining chapel.

Nola would've appreciated that an abundant, piping hot, aromatic lunch was delivered too early to serve, and that because it would've gotten cold if we waited, my brother Mike and Gail and I decided to feed the guests before we started her service. Priorities.

I believe the funeral parlor may have given us a volume discount or maybe a pity discount as Nola's was the third of three funerals in our immediate family in the span of a little over three years.

We decorated the funeral parlor for the first time with a sense of shock when I lost my husband Al to cancer three months after What Would Nola Do? was published in 2014. Al, the father of my children, the chef extraordinaire, the man who I think believed in me more than he believed in himself. Al's death was not supposed to happen. In hindsight, Al's effortless but noticeable weight loss over time, the chronic exhaustion, the strange back pain and the odd tan, which turned out to be the yellowing skin color of jaundice, should not have been downplayed, should not have been seen as isolated symptoms, but rather the markings of cancer - bile duct cancer, deep in his pancreas, found too late to treat successfully. Diagnosed in June, gone in October. Al's mother and sister, my Courtney, Nic and I decorated the funeral parlor for the first time with Al's collection of Philadelphia Phillies and Eagles' memorabilia, lots of photos of family, copies of the newspapers he read every day, and lots of Kit Kat bars, his favorite.

As Nola used to say, "The old must die, the young may die." My children lost their devoted, loving, fun and funny father. I lost what I felt like was my right arm. Our house would go up for sale a year later. It was just too hard to be there without Al. It was quietly comforting to see Joe, one of James's brothers, paying his respects at Al's funeral. How nice to sense James's presence. I visited his mother once or twice a year after James's passing in 2010, his portrait prominently displayed at the entrance of her home, I felt like he was watching over her. And I bet he was.

My father, Lloyd, attended my husband's funeral that fall of 2014. This was not the natural order as my father was 36 years older than Al. Both men had cancer. Daddy would pass the following year, another Anderson living into his 90s, but living the last two years alone in the home he and Nola shared after moving from the Bronx to a 55 and older community in 1997. No longer safe in their little ranch house in this gated community, despite our vigilance and eventually the live-in helper - God bless long-term care insurance - Mike, Gail and I reluctantly moved Nola to a dementia unit in a high rise five minutes from me, an hour from my brother, two hours from my sister. Dementia took Nola's freedom. Dementia took Nola's home. Dementia took the memories of what just happened moments before while leaving the past quite clearly intact.

Nola moved from a walker to a wheelchair, from panties to diapers, from solids to puree. But she always recognized her family, even when she wasn't too happy to see us. Nola could answer any trivia question offered during group games at her unit, but agonized over what she knew she didn't know and couldn't do anymore. My father asked us not to empty all the clothes from Nola's closet, just in case she was coming back. She never did.

My father, Lloyd, was diagnosed with lung cancer at 90. He opted not to seek treatment as he and his doctor agreed that he had had a good run. And the tests and medical invasions of his days were not a good use of the time he had left. Daddy's days would be spent doing what he always did, puttering, fixing, playing solitaire, tinkering with watches as he had throughout his working years, and new to what he always did, visiting my lady, Nola, every weekend, courtesy of one or more of his children in the role of chauffer.

Out from behind Nola's big personality, Mike and Gail and I found our father enjoying the attention, embracing his days as he slowly faded. Lloyd's last family event was his granddaughter Megan's wedding in July of 2015. We all doted on him as he marveled at the look and sound of the first live band he'd probably ever seen. A week later at 92, Daddy walked with my brother into a Hospice located in a cottage behind the local hospital. On the first night, Daddy decided he didn't like his room, gathered his belongings and moved them to a bigger room. On the second night, Daddy stealthily made his way to the top of the back stairs, but was thankfully stopped by a nurse. On the third night, Daddy went to sleep for the last time.

The funeral parlor was again decorated with our memories, and his brother and fellow car aficionado blew the horn - his Klaxon "Ahooga" horn, restored by my brother Mike. Lloyd arrived in New York from Jamaica in 1960 with his new wife Nola by his side, and his Klaxon horn on his lap. The horn that announced his arrival and exit for every visit of my life was blown one last time as the room shared a rum punch toast.

Nola, too, left this life in a way that felt like Nola, especially when she told us not to go to too much trouble even over something this big. The last time I saw my mother alive I truly wondered if it was gonna be my last time. Uncharacteristically quiet, her appetite distressingly poor, her body curled downward in her wheelchair, I turned up Tom Jones's *"It's Not Unusual"* to keep Nola awake long enough to get in a few bites of lunch. I wheeled her to her room, where for the first time I'd ever seen it, the nurses whose task was to keep the residents engaged and busy, simply let Nola lie down in her bed and rest. I helplessly winced at my mother's pain as they gently supported her into lying down. I left for a guilty weekend away from her for my first wedding anniversary. More on that later.

Nola died the day after that anniversary, and I missed the call from the unit, me, the first contact on the list, the one who lived five minutes away. My sister in New York received the call and contacted me with the news. Nola, our mother, our little mummy-du, our "Mu" was gone. Did Nola wait until I was away to pass on? Did Nola wait until the day after my anniversary so as not to taint that happy day with sadness? Perhaps Nola preferred a simple, quiet exit. Didn't want us to go to too much trouble. I imagine her brother, the one whose passing broke her heart and started her dementia, depression decline, so long ago, welcoming her home.

Sometimes I wonder if, uh, after being freed from those well-worn 90-something-year-old bodies, Nola and Lloyd sent my brother Mike and Gail and me some little thank you gifts. Perhaps Nola and Lloyd thought the three of us might enjoy some personalized blessings in their absence, as it felt like each of us was ripe for change after so much loss. For Mike, I think the blessing was the sale of the home he had on the market for far too long, the gift of moving forward to a new state, to a new urban lifestyle that would be very different from the suburbs in a way Mike and his wife were surprised to enjoy as much as they do. For Gail, I feel like she was blessed with the anchor of an administrative position at the college she attended years before, that would provide her the stability, and sometimes the headaches, to be able to combine her long and remarkable career as a leader in graphic design with, let's be honest, healthcare and retirement benefits. For me - and this is a little embarrassing - I think Nola and my dad sent a man, Michael.

I found love again with a big, silver haired, football obsessed, IT guy with a heart of gold, three young adult children of his own, and lots of hard opinions on retirement planning. A new husband at my age? Me? With two young adults in the house, one with a disability and all the issues that come with it? With this hair? And with what so many cookies did to this waistline? Yes. Michael and I married in 2017, and Nola didn't leave a sad memory on my happy day by dying on my first anniversary. Thank you, "Mu."

The parlor for Nola's funeral service was decorated with photos, photo albums, her souvenirs of her favorite cartoon character, Snoopy, bowls of her ever-present Starlight Mints, and a lot of other doo-dads that felt like "Mu." We were pretty good at decorating that funeral parlor after our two prior efforts. Mike delivered the eulogy, saying he couldn't have asked for a better stepmother. Goose bump moment.

Born on the same day in June, Mike and Nola shared the humor and the temperament of the Gemini, the welcomer, the warrior, the juggler. To strangers, Nola and Mike often physically passed for mother and son, even though they weren't - at least not by blood.

After the service - perhaps as a way of saying grace over the food - Gail and I decided to pay tribute to our mother's many thoughts on how to live your life by reciting a little list called *10 Things I Learned from Nola* which we thought sounded clever. True to Nola's many hard opinions and gentle wisdom, there were, of course, more than 10 things she would habitually remind us all. I hope I've passed even some of these little pearls on to my Courtney and Nic, and maybe Courtney will pass them on to her own children too.

So I present this list to you now as, *What Would Nola Say?* Simple but true, Nola's family lives by these words to this day.

One, keep in touch. Write letters, call, text, email, send cards, be a friend.

Two, "ring twice and hang up." Back in the day when you had a landline, but "ring twice and hangup" when you get home kinda said, "Look out for the people you love and let them know you're okay." Ringing twice and hanging up, you didn't even have to say anything, you just knew that call meant, "I'm okay."

Three, be thoughtful. Bring cookies when the nurses are nice. Be there when needed without having to be asked.

Four, make sure everyone eats, even if you don't like to cook.

Five, try to keep your faith, even if you don't always get to church.

Six, enjoy a laugh. In her day, it was Flip Wilson, Dane Edna, Bob and Ray, Snoopy. But now it's whoever you find funny.

Number *seven*, read and read and read. Learn. Be amused. Get opinionated, but read.

Eight, be prepared. Make sure you always have batteries, tissues and gum.

Nine, touch your toes. In other words, get some exercise.

Ten, remember to water your plants, even though you may accidentally kill them.

Eleven, make sure you have your eyebrows on. That was never my problem, but what she was saying was, "You never know who's gonna show up."

Twelve, play the numbers and buy lottery tickets because someone's gotta win that money.

Thirteen, swear sometimes. Dammit!

Fourteen, don't go to too much trouble. Simple is okay too.

And finally, number *fifteen*, make sure your hair looks good. I think for me, that's the hardest one.

2024...

I think Nola would be proud of her legacy. Gail, Mike and I miss her still. Nola's name remains a part of the conversation, the memories, and stories and lessons our mother left us. Her grandchildren, Meg, Nic, Courtney and Jacob, remember Nola was love, a smile, and a story or two of something she said or did.

Would Nola have been proud of Courtney's completion of six years of service in the Navy? I know she would have had something to say about being proud but also being astonished that Courtney was sworn in to this bit of "unbelievable," at Fort Dix just a few miles from Nola's home. And don't even mention (it didn't stop there) Courtney's deployment to the Persian Gulf. I'm betting Nola would have written her every day.

Would Nola burst with pride that Nic is working four days a week in the community, and lives with his buddy and supports in my old condo? Or that he helps out with the kids at Sunday school class every week? That Nic goes out on the occasional date? Like I'd have to ask.

Nola has great grandchildren now, 8 and counting. And I count my own first granddaughter Viviana among them because Courtney's impulsive elopement is going strong at 5 years and counting. My mother would have loved that. And Nola would have been there for all of these children, each in their own way as she always was for Gail, and Mike, and me.

About the Author

Always mom first, now a grandmother as well, Dr. Geralyn Anderson Arango is a Professor of Education, Emerita at Holy Family University in Philadelphia, PA. Gerry writes, teaches and consults on topics pertaining to intellectual disability across all phases of life. Gerry is the host of *"Our Parallel Paths: A Future for My Loved One with a Disability… and For Me!"* a podcast produced by Networks for Training and Development.

Gerry lives in Wilmington, Delaware with her husband Michael, and hopes that their imminent retirement won't make them weirder than their cats.

Want to hear more from this author?
Connect with Gerry on her podcast, *"Our Parallel Paths: A Future for My Loved One with a Disability… and for Me!"*, and join the conversation on Facebook at *What Would Nola Do* and *Our Parallel Paths: A Future for My Loved One with a Disability… & for Me*. Stay tuned for more insights, stories, and behind-the-scenes content!